Ga...
Messages

MESSAGES FROM
THE ARCHANGEL GABRIEL

First published by O Books, 2008
O Books is an imprint of John Hunt Publishing Ltd., The Bothy, Deershot Lodge, Park Lane, Ropley,
Hants, SO24 0BE, UK
office1@o-books.net
www.o-books.net

Distribution in:

UK and Europe
Orca Book Services
orders@orcabookservices.co.uk
Tel: 01202 665432 Fax: 01202 666219
Int. code (44)

USA and Canada
NBN
custserv@nbnbooks.com
Tel: 1 800 462 6420 Fax: 1 800 338 4550

Australia and New Zealand
Brumby Books
sales@brumbybooks.com.au
Tel: 61 3 9761 5535 Fax: 61 3 9761 7095

Far East (offices in Singapore, Thailand,
Hong Kong, Taiwan)
Pansing Distribution Pte Ltd
kemal@pansing.com
Tel: 65 6319 9939 Fax: 65 6462 5761

South Africa
Alternative Books
altbook@peterhyde.co.za
Tel: 021 555 4027 Fax: 021 447 1430

Text copyright Shanta Gabriel 2008

Design: Stuart Davies

ISBN: 978 1 84694 159 7

All rights reserved. Except for brief quotations
in critical articles or reviews, no part of this
book may be reproduced in any manner without
prior written permission from the publishers.

The rights of Shanta Gabriel as author have
been asserted in accordance with the
Copyright, Designs and Patents Act 1988.

A CIP catalogue record for this book is available
from the British Library.

Printed in the UK by CPI Antony Rowe, Chippenham, Wiltshire

O Books operates a distinctive and ethical publishing philosophy in
all areas of its business, from its global network of authors to
production and worldwide distribution.
This book is produced on FSC certified stock, within ISO14001
standards. The printer plants sufficient trees each year through
the Woodland Trust to absorb the level of emitted carbon in
its production.

The Gabriel Messages

MESSAGES FROM
THE ARCHANGEL GABRIEL

Shanta Gabriel

West Bend Public Library
630 Poplar Street
West Bend, WI 53095
262-335-5151
www.west-bendlibrary.org/

BOOKS

Winchester, UK
Washington, USA

Contents

Acknowledgements

This book is a revised version of *Angel Messages Book and Card Set* published in 1997. After the book went out of print, I was surprised and blessed by how many people called wanting a copy. So many people contacted me over the years to tell me how their hearts had been touched, and how life changing they found these compassionate words from Archangel Gabriel, that I knew it was time to reach out again with the Light-filled blessings this book carries. I am grateful to John Hunt and O-Books for making this possible. *The Gabriel Messages* were created out of my desire to empower people with simple, practical and uplifting support in their daily lives. Calling on the timeless wisdom of the Angels brings us closer to the inner peace we long for and the joy we deserve. As before, this book is still dedicated to Peace on Earth one person at a time.

Shanta Gabriel, 2008

The Purpose and Use of *The Gabriel Messages*

Today over six billion people walk the continents of this earth. Every day we face the traumatic and disturbing details of our news reports. Without an understanding of the true nature of our world, we could easily lose sight of the possibility for human beings to live in peace, harmony and abundance.

If our goal is to see this reality made manifest in our individual and collective lives, how might we contribute to achieving such an earthly paradise? I believe we can begin by looking beyond the outer shell of our human form to a Higher Power at work. Moving past the restricting thought-forms of the outer world, we can sense the inner pulse of life and know its purest nature.

The Infinite Intelligence that stands behind all creation has been called by many names. This omnipresent principle of light and wisdom shines through each of us regardless of our socio-economic situation, level of understanding, or current place in our soul's journey. When we consciously seek clarity and the grace of Divine awareness, we join in harmony with this ultimate Universal Presence.

Through the ages great philosophers have spoken of the benefits of group prayer and meditation. A critical mass of dedicated people uniting in prayer to bless the planet and bring heavenly Light into their lives cannot help but produce benevolent outcomes in the overall human experience. These blessings, and even miracles, multiply through Divine Love, and flow out to connect the body, mind and spirit of the prayer-giver with all of Life.

This earth is a manifestation of heavenly design and purpose, and I see our mission in physical life as being a bridge for helping to bring the light of Heaven to Earth. Each day we have the opportunity to share in this glorious undertaking through the choices we make in thought, word and action. Seeking daily inspiration to help us make the optimal choices for our highest good is the first step.

You may find *The Gabriel Messages* a helpful focus for quiet prayer times and meditation. They are easy to understand and may be used in a variety of ways. Whenever a situation develops which requires an expanded perspective for resolution, hold the intention for clarity in your mind, and open the book anywhere. The message on the chosen page will guide your mind into a new, helpful direction. At times you may not be seeking a particular answer to a personal challenge, but may feel a need for heightened spiritual awareness. You may be worried about a loved one or a friend, or you may need to focus your energy on a specific task throughout a busy day. Whatever your need may be, the message you choose can help bring the peace, comfort and tangible direction required in your current situation.

In order to bring more harmony to the earth as well as our individual lives it is important to find our own way to pray and meditate every day. In this way we can lift our spirits and be in touch with the Light and Love of God's Presence moving within our lives moment by moment. When our intention is only to receive that which is in the highest good for ourselves and all concerned, we will attract to us only what will best serve that purpose.

May those who read *The Gabriel Messages* be blessed by the Angels and held in wings of Divine Love. May all live in harmony, joy, peace and abundance. Through God's Grace may all beings achieve the highest good for all of Creation.

And so it is.

Shanta Gabriel, 2008

The Balanced Breath

Developing a place of silence within yourself, a peaceful center where you are aware of the Presence of God, is the most important and useful gift you can give yourself in these rapidly changing times. The easiest way to become centered is to use the breath as a focusing tool. Your breath is your connection to the Divine Source, so never belittle the simplicity of breathing in a focused, conscious manner.

Many of the messages in this book contain Practices that refer to the balanced breath. Balanced breathing is simply breathing in for the same number of counts that you breathe out. If you can hold your breath for the same number of counts, between breathing in and out, this will help increase the effectiveness. It is said that God lives in this space between the breaths.

Choose a number that is easy for you, such as four or seven. Breathe in for four counts, hold for four counts, exhale for four counts, and hold out for four counts. This seems very simple, and yet you will find yourself becoming calm and peaceful as you do this practice. It is important to begin with an intention or a prayer to connect deeply with God, and to have a conscious connection with your Higher Self. This sets energy in motion so you will receive good results.

While you are sitting quietly and breathing, you can use your imagination to gain awareness of Divine Love waiting to fill you up with the living life-force energy. As you inhale, imagine that every cell in your being is filled with God's light, and is radiantly alive. Imagine, on your exhalation, that you are releasing everything within you that is not in harmony with your greater good. Your imagination is the first step in creating what you want in your life and is a very powerful tool.

If you would like to have a peaceful place to come to whenever you wish to be centered, with your imagination you can create a garden, a beautiful room or a place in nature for your special meditation space. With practice, you can come to this place in your mind on your first breath and stay there until you feel more calm and relaxed.

It is also important to create a connection between Heaven and Earth, so that you can bring back this new, centered awareness to your daily life. One way to accomplish this is to imagine a huge pillar of golden light bringing God's love into your body and then through you into the earth. You can use this visualization whenever you start to feel off-center during the day. It will help to bring you back to that peaceful place you have developed within you through the use of the balanced breath technique.

The Power of Intention

There are moments in our lives when declaring our intention becomes life defining. It is different than reciting our material goals. Intention draws to us the qualities we want manifested in our lives. It has been said that we can know our intentions by the results we see around us. The power of intention works whether it is conscious or not. During this time of accelerated growth and planting of seeds, making a conscious statement about what qualities we are choosing for our lives is paramount.

Many years ago I was taught an ancient statement called the *Diamond Covenant of Moses* which states to the Universe, "I will do whatever is impressed upon me without a shadow of a doubt." It calls to our Angels to bring messages about our lives into a stronger statement of being. This means asking for clarity and strength in the inner guidance we are receiving all the time.

When we can direct our intention into a greater level of planetary service, or into qualities such as Wisdom, Joy and Peace, the vibrational frequency around us quickens. This not only enriches our lives directly, it affects the amount of Light on the planet from moment to moment.

Once we make a statement of Intention to the Universe, this clarity of focus is released. It begins to work in the energy around us and manifest directly in our world. An intention is like the arrow sent directly to the Creator of our lives. When we create a powerful statement of intention, it is doing our part as if pulling back the string of the bow and releasing our arrow to manifest the creative solutions we are truly capable of.

Never before has there been a time when the Power of Intention is so strong. Know in your heart that all your needs are met with grace and ease. Be very clear about what you are willing to give back to a Universe for a life filled with Good.

Do not forget the grace that comes with gratitude. Remember

to give thanks for the wondrous gift of life. All that you give is blessed and returned to you multiplied. Clarify your intentions. Make a covenant with God now. The Angels await your call to action.

The Gabriel Messages #1

Gently and with love, honor yourself.

Dear One,

You are sometimes kinder to total strangers than you are to yourself. You are a magnificent being of light. Honor and remember this for it is not easy to be in an earth body. There are many demands on you. You can be so involved with day-to-day struggles that you do not feel you have time to remember your spirit. And yet it is the focus on your spirit that will make your earth-walk easier.

Honor yourself in gentleness and love. You are not alone. The Infinite Presence has not placed you onto the earth plane without a way of receiving assistance when you most need it. That is why there are Angels. Angels are messengers from God who are here to assist in making your earthly life more effortless, to bring light into the darkness, and to remind you that you are incredibly loved.

We know of your struggle, and we know that you are making a valiant effort. We bless you and honor you for all that you have done and are doing. But more than that, we honor you for who you are deep inside. We honor that part of you which is the essence of the light of Spirit. We see within you a spark of incredible goodness and love. This we bless and honor and we urge you to do the same. The more you bless and honor this Divine Light within you, the more it grows. The more this light grows, the more love you feel and the more energy you have. The more love you feel within you, the more you want to give to others. In this way the world is served and more light is brought to your beautiful planet, which is in need of great blessings at this time.

We ask you to be gentle with yourself, to be as kind to yourself as you are to others. Without love and encouragement a little child cannot grow to be a healthy adult. Yet you never outgrow your need for love and, remember, it is important to give yourself this love first, before you can fully give it to others.

Practice

How does one love oneself? You can start with the small things. Say, "I love you" to yourself whenever you look into a mirror. Remember to give yourself daily acknowledgment for how hard you work, for how much effort you give to another, for how caring you are to your children. For whatever you can think of, acknowledge yourself. If you cannot think of anything, simply acknowledge yourself for getting through another day on earth and doing the best you can do. As simple as this may seem, it is very powerful.

The most important way you can love and honor yourself is by remembering who you are deep inside – a radiant spirit of light growing stronger and more whole every day. This is the truth of you. You can love yourself by eating in healthy ways and doing all that you know serves your body, but true loving and honoring begins with your thoughts about yourself. You are here on earth to express spirit in form and to learn to be loving, joyful and peaceful. It does no good to berate yourself because you are not yet perfectly expressing these qualities. You were not given a manual for life on earth, so the only way you can learn is through trial and error, and by often painful experiences which encourage you to grow through the choices you make. You are doing just fine. Please honor this.

There are many ways you can gently love and honor yourself. We ask you to give yourself kindness and compassion, to do the best you can with all aspects of your life, and to call on a Higher Power to assist you at all times, no matter how mundane the situation. The Angels are Divine messengers here to help you, bless you and, most of all, to love you. Receive love and remember to:

gently and with love, honor yourself.

The Gabriel Messages #2

You are always receiving God's love whether you "tune in" or not.

Dear One,

God's love is the energy that permeates the universe. It is the essence in which you live and move and have your being. There is no time when you are separate from this Divine Love, whether or not you are aware of this fact. Divine Love is always there for you.

If you do choose to be aware that you are basking in the light of the universe in every moment, your life can change for the better. When you remember that you are always receiving God's blessings, you can know that you are supremely loved. No matter what you have done, or not done, you are loved. No matter how imperfect you feel, you are loved. You are the beloved child of a benevolent Spirit who wants you to be happy, free, wealthy and filled with love. This is what you deserve because you are you.

You have come to this place and time to hear this message. You need to remember how much your life is worth to the Creator of all that is. Bask in this possibility for a moment. Breathe in the Divine Light and know, really know, how much you are loved.

There is no one else in the world with the gifts, talents and abilities that you have. When you realize this, you can give thanks, knowing the way is now open for you to use your God-given talents and abilities to expand and enrich your life. For this you came to earth.

You also came to earth to learn the lessons you have chosen to learn. These lessons may feel difficult. You may see no way to accomplish your dreams. You may not even feel as though it is okay to have your dreams. Yet within you there is a spark of light that believes that you are receiving Divine love.

This love, which you are continuously receiving, holds the energy that can carry your dreams into the world. This love can heal all that causes you pain. This love brings hope and carries the seed of truth within its light-filled energy. It's here for you now. Breathe in Divine Love.

The Angels are messengers of God. They carry Divine Love to those who will listen and receive all that is available to them from the Universal Presence. So ask to receive this love. You are worthy to have the love of God in every area of your life.

Remember as you go through this day, no matter what you are doing or where you are:

you are always receiving God's love, whether you "tune in" or not.

The Gabriel Messages #3

Your way to Harmony is remembering who you are in every moment...a Divine Expression, Spirit into matter.

Dear One,

Who you are is so much more than a body in the material world. Your very essence is part of a greater whole – God in whom you live, move and have your being, the Source of all Life.

This Presence expressing through you is the gift you give to the world. Imagine what earth would be like if all people remembered they were the Divine Essence expressing in a physical world. There would be so much love, and so little fear. In the essence of God, there is no separation into race or religion. There is no separation of any kind. It is all a great whole.

When you remember that you truly are spirit and your purpose is to bring God through you into the physical world, different choices can be made. In the world of spirit, love, compassion and trust are key elements. In the world of spirit, joy, harmony and peace exist in all situations. There is freedom in your mind when you allow this truth to be in the forefront of your consciousness.

Release the need to believe as others do. Be the one who remembers God and speaks the truth. Be the one who blesses the world with the power of your remembering. If it is not appropriate to speak this truth, silently bless all people and situations when they are brought to your awareness. You will be a powerful force for good.

When you find others who are in agreement with you, and who know the truth of their Divine Expression, pray together. The power of remembering truth when two or more are gathered, creates an exponential leap of love and light in the world. Join together in a conspiracy of love to bless all people and situations where fear is the predominant emotion. Many people believe there are better ways to live than what is apparent in the cities of the world. Many have withdrawn to lead separate lives. Never doubt the power of one. One person can bring tremendous good to the world when acting from the consciousness of greater truth and love.

The energy of loving prayer and blessings strengthens the link all people share – oneness with God. When more people send love, blessings and prayers toward others, the very vibration of the planet is increased. An increase in vibration stimulates more love and light. Harmony, peace and more love are then generated.

This is the way to heal the world – moment to moment, each person blessing others and bringing love into every situation, instead of fear. These actions not only assist all beings, they renew our faith in a benevolent and loving Presence within all things, thus all are healed.

Remember,

your way to Harmony is by remembering who you are in every moment...a Divine Expression, Spirit into matter.

The Gabriel Messages #4

You are never far from the Light. It is as close as your breath.

Dear One,

Your breath is your connection to God. Breathing is the first thing you do when you arrive on earth, and the last as you depart. Your breath feeds your body and mind the oxygen it needs to exist. Your breath also holds the power to create an expansion in your energy so you can be aware of your link to the Source of all life.

Divine Light is showering upon you at all times and it radiates from within your being to the world around you. This light holds the essence of peace and love. The more you are aware of your connection to this light, the happier you become.

There are times when you may feel alone and in turmoil because of situations in your life. It is at these times that breathing consciously and remembering the light of God will be helpful. When you pray to experience the power of your connection to the Divine Presence, you are opening a door in your mind to allow in more light. The more you open, the more you are flooded with light and love. Remember at these times that your breath is the key to opening this door.

Practice

When you breathe in a conscious manner, taking in and releasing balanced breaths, it will compose your energy and allow you to focus on God. Continue to breathe and pray for greater awareness of Divine Presence in your

life at all times. Ask to know your oneness with the Divine as you breathe deeply, and anxiety will drop away. It is difficult to be upset when you are breathing deeply and openly. Part of your anxiousness is caused from breathing very shallow breaths. Your body starts to fear that it won't receive enough oxygen to live, so taking a few moments to breathe in a conscious way is very reassuring to your body as well as your mind.

As you inhale, imagine you are breathing in the light of God and allowing it to flow into every cell of your being. As you breathe out, imagine that you are releasing everything within you that is not of your highest good. Each breath renews you. As the light creates more clarity and focus, Divine Love brings you peace.

Remember that you are never alone. There are messengers from God in the form of Angels who are available always to bring you peace and guidance. You can call on the Angels and ask to know personally your guiding Angelic presence. Prayer is always answered. You can ask for what you want to be or to have in your life, knowing that it will manifest for your highest good. You can release to the Angels all that no longer serves you. Then give yourself time to breathe and receive the abundant level of love and wisdom carried by Divine Light.

Your life will change in miraculous ways when you remember:

you are never far from the Light. It is as close as your breath.

The Gabriel Messages #5

Resonate with what is true for you and leave the rest.

Dear One,

Every day you receive wisdom and guidance from the Angels. Sometimes this guidance comes from those around you – friends, family, teachers, strangers or signs in obvious places. Sometimes this wisdom comes as an inner urging. Whenever you receive guidance, if you tune within, you will feel a resonance when it is coming from a place of truth. Call this your "God check." Create your own little sign that you can recognize when something is right for you. Then you have a way to really know what it is in your highest good at all times.

It is important to do this "God check" before your mental activity is engaged because the mind creates confusion at times. It is the heart that is in tune with Infinite Intelligence. This is where you receive your truth. Many times what is in your highest good may not be the most rational of acts. You must be willing to do that which resonates deep within as the most appropriate action for you to take.

The Divine Guidance within you knows the answers. Before you can hear them, however, it may take a little prayer you make to yourself in moments of decision, especially when you are receiving conflicting advice from many well-meaning people around you. Take the time to center within, so you can know what is true for you.

Practice

One little ritual that may be helpful for you is to stop, take a deep breath, and say to yourself: "the Divine Guidance within me knows the truth in this situation." Take several deep breaths and continue with your life process. You will feel a resonance within

..self that is your true knowing. The more you act on this resonance, the stronger it will become. Be willing more and more to do that which your heart tells you is right for you, rather than following your rational thoughts or the suggestions of those around you.

No one knows more than you do what is truly in your highest good, when you are in that infinite connection to the Source of all life. Ask for this connection to be strong and clear.

It is very helpful to give thanks in advance for clear direction from God. This creates a frequency of energy within and around you that allows the Angels to bring you assistance. An attitude of gratitude goes a long way to bring about that which you most want in your life. Be clear about the qualities you want – such as joy, wisdom, love, prosperity and peace. All of these qualities represent the energy of the universe that is always available to you. You must ask for them directly in order to receive them. You also need to keep bringing your focus of attention back to what you want, rather than focusing on what you don't want in your life.

So the steps we are suggesting in order to bring about a higher level of order in your life are:

Stop, breathe, ask, give thanks and then be willing to receive on a level you have never believed possible. Allow the universal energy of the Angels to work in your life.

When you come from this high level of intention, you will begin to sense within you the resonance of your highest truth. And from this place comes Divine Right Action. Remember your message from the Angels today:

resonate with what is true for you and leave the rest.

The Gabriel Messages #6

This is the time for those who believe to let go of fear and reach their hand forward, to be held and led by the Angels of Light.

Dear One,

When you resolve to let go of fear, an amazing energy is set into motion. It is as though hands of Angels join together in circles of light around you, keeping you protected and nurtured. When you walk, you are carried by these Angels "lest you strike your foot against a stone," as is said in Psalm 91.

Sometimes letting go of fear can feel as though you are walking off a cliff. It is often necessary to take this large step in order to make the greatest progress in your life. When your intention is to serve the Highest Good in all you do, and when you have the willingness to move through your fear of the unknown, this step off a cliff will be into the arms of these magnificent beings of light. Angels will assist you to fly to the heights of grandeur and to the depths of peace.

The saying "there is nothing to fear but fear itself" is true. Fear can play in your imagination until you are immobilized. From this place you can easily sink into the pits of despair. It will feel as though you are not moving toward your destiny, and that is the most fear-filled place of all. This fear will play upon your issues of worthiness, because in your heart you want most of all to add value to the world.

Know truly that you were created to be happy. Feeling joy is one of the greatest tasks you have in your life. You are here to do great things, and this can be as simple as loving others and bringing more peace and joy to the world. When you have joy as your intention, you will be shown what you have to do.

Practice

Take some time to sit quietly and breathe in a balanced way. Imagine that you are standing on a mountain top. It is the highest peak around you. It is so high that eagles are flying below where you are standing. There is a magnificent sunrise lighting up the sky and surrounding your body with golden light.

From this pinnacle of light, you offer yourself to serve God in the world and you ask for courage to do whatever it takes. Call on the Angels for assistance to be all you can be. At this moment you hear the sound of wings and you notice the light becoming even brighter. You are surrounded by Angels and you feel your fear melting with their love. They are holding out their hands to you. It is such a reach to touch them, it is difficult to keep your footing. In order to touch the hands of the Angels, you know you are going to have to take a step off the cliff. You feel all the old fears beginning to surface again. This time, you will not give in to fear. Your conviction to have love and joy in your life and to serve in the world is greater than the fear.

You take a deep breath, and look into the eyes of the Angels surrounding you. You see a hand of light reaching toward you and a beaming presence of love smiling at you. The Angels are saying they believe in you, they love you, and know you can do whatever you want. In this moment you know that the safety of that which is familiar cannot bring you the joy and the power of love you are feeling from the Angels. Looking at the hands being offered, you let the love you are feeling in your heart uplift you, and you reach your own hands toward the Angels of Light. You take the first step.

In this moment of freefall, your heart begins to pound. But it is only an instant before arms hold you and you feel yourself being transported into the light. The Angels are taking you with them. Let yourself imagine what it would be like to fly with the Angels. Feel the warmth of the sun, the wind in your hair and let yourself be held and led where they will take you. Know in your heart it is to your greatest good. Allow yourself to fly with the Angels. Feel the freedom that is there for you and let Divine Love fill your heart.

Take a look at where you are held back by fear, and see the darkness there. Are you willing to have it be different now? There is help for you. Angelic assistance is available. This simple visualization exercise can have miraculous results. It is your choice to take the first step by being willing to have a miracle change your life.

It is time for you to decide. Do you want to serve God and let the Angels help you fly? Are you willing to have miracles and joy fill your life? Do you believe miracles are possible and Angels exist? If your answer is yes – know that...

this is the time for those who believe to let go of fear and reach their hand forward to be held and led by the Angels of Light.

The Gabriel Messages #7

*Feeling free to be yourself is the greatest gift
you can give.*

Dear One,

In your heart you are free. This energy of freedom can be expressed in your daily life as well as kept as a sacred trust within you. This energy is God working through you and encouraging you to let your light shine.

When you are feeling free to be yourself, that is the time your light shines the brightest. That is when you are most relaxed and happy, which is the way your Spirit intended you to live.

When you let your light shine in the world, darkness is illuminated. The parts of society that offer the greatest challenge are the ones needing the most light. Allowing God's love to pour through you as Divine Light is one of the best ways to create the changes you want in your world. This energy of love-filled light can bring wholeness and healing to any situation.

When you come to this place of light within you, it reminds you of the joyous state of a happy child. You are being encouraged to express this joyous energy in your family and worldly life. It is the spontaneous freedom to speak the truth from your heart with kindness and compassion. It is the enthusiasm to do what you most want to do, knowing that you are divinely inspired in every moment. These are the gifts you are being asked to give to the world.

Experience the freedom of Divine Light at work within you. Feel free to ask for so much love to come through you that you can let it overflow to others. Ask for abundant joy within you so that you can share it. Ask to speak your highest truth with the compassion of the Angels. Ask to really know in your heart that which is right for you to do and say. Ask to be a vehicle of light moving in the world. All this gives you perfect freedom of expression while knowing the divine resources within you at all times.

You are a gift to the world when you express all of the beauty inside you. Share your most sacred self when you feel the guidance to do so. Allow God's light to shine through you and remember:

feeling free to be yourself is the greatest gift you can give.

The Gabriel Messages #8

When you dedicate your life to God you move into the lifestream of Pure Consciousness where there are no limitations.

Dear One,

When you dedicate your life to God, an expansion occurs. When your energy fields expand, the limitations of the physical world begin to drop away. You feel lighter, uplifted and more joyful. Your heart resonates at a deeper level of truth. You begin to operate at a higher level of awareness. This new awareness brings you a more enlightened perspective on your life.

It is a wondrous feeling to be in a place of enlightened perspective. All of a sudden you look at your world with new eyes. Your attitude is one of love and compassion, and you become more forgiving of situations that would normally have upset you. This is the grace available to you from the Divine Source. It is always available to you and exists as a stream of heightened energy-frequency, or Pure Consciousness.

How do you reach this heightened state of awareness? Through prayer and communion with your Higher Self, by connecting to the loving Source of all that is, and by breaking free of the bonds which limit your thoughts and conscious awareness of life.

So many people contain their thoughts in limiting boxes. Because things appear to be a certain way, they believe it to be truth. The Angels are here to show you another way of looking at life, one in which there always exists a greater level of truth, and where love and harmony are the qualities you can manifest. When you breathe deeply and visualize your energy-field expanding, you are allowing this greater level of truth to become apparent to you. It becomes even easier if you ask your guardian Angel to show it to you. Asking is a form of prayer, and there is opportunity available to see the "larger picture" if you want to. Prayers are always answered.

When you pray you open the door for a greater level of energy to work in your life. This is the pure potential energy that becomes available to you as you turn your life over to God. We call it a Lifestream because this is the energy in which you live, move and have your being. It is the essence of you, because you are a part of All that Is. When you remember this truth, and give yourself time to commune with the Higher Power within you, limitations drop away.

Practice

Right now, take the time to dedicate your life to God. Imagine this Lifestream of pure consciousness flowing around and through you in rivers of love and light. Be willing to have your limiting beliefs drop away so that miracles can occur for you in your physical world. Sometimes it might appear as though only a miracle can make the difference in your situation. Allow this to occur as the natural result of remembering the Divine Spirit that is really in charge of your life. The Angels are available to assist you, as close as a prayer. Open yourself to a new way of seeing your world where love, joy and harmony abound. All this is possible when you remember your Angel message today.

when you dedicate your life to God you move into the life stream of Pure Consciousness where there are no limitations.

The Gabriel Messages #9

Trust in the Divine Plan, bless it and bless the Divine Order inherent in every person and every situation.

Dear One,

When you trust in the Divine Plan you are moving into the universal flow of good. You are acknowledging that there is an underlying energy within all things. This is the energy of God, and it is part of the Divine Plan for all beings to live in harmony, love and abundance. You can trust this.

When you bless the Divine Order inherent in every person and every situation, it increases the spiritual energy flowing through whatever you are focused upon. Blessing brings more love to the person or situation, which brings an immediate improvement.

Practice

Divine Order exists as the underlying truth within all beings and all situations. It is a powerful affirmation for life and can be used as a mantra to remind you of the greater truth within all circumstances. This means repeating the words "divine order" to settle your mind, and to bring you peace. When you don't know what to do, claim "divine order" and your mind will align with this powerful reality. Divine Order is being in perfect alignment with God on every level of your being. Remembering Divine Order, and proclaiming it, assists the energy around you to fall into perfect alignment.

These very simple steps of trusting, blessing and remembering can bring you peace of mind in upsetting situations. The more often you remember, the stronger you become. Your inner sense of peace will become unshakable because you have aligned yourself with the ultimate truth at all times. Remember your message from the Angels today:

trust in the Divine Plan, bless it and bless the Divine Order inherent in every person and every situation.

The Gabriel Messages #10

Loving others in their own chosen path is setting the energy you want in your world.

Dear One,

When you love others and allow them to follow their own chosen path, it awakens the energy of compassion and acceptance within you. This energy fills your heart and permeates your world. It allows you to receive this same energy from others, which can give you a sense of freedom to be all you can be.

At times the chosen path of others may seem destructive to you, and it is not the energy that you would choose to be around. In these situations, often the most loving thing you can do is allow them to follow their chosen path, and you must give yourself permission to follow the path which is in your highest good. This may even mean never seeing them again.

Set the energy you want in your world by awakening your consciousness to all the good available to you. It's a matter of choice. Attune yourself to only that which you would have in your life. Release the need to be right. Close your mind to the negative thoughts that threaten your happiness. Moment to moment, make the choice to live in the light of love. This is being a true bridge from Heaven to Earth. Making the choice for love allows you to be in the world but not of the world. When you make the choice to love others as they are, you pave the way for a mass awakening of love on the planet so all may be free.

Receive love, give love and be love. With this loving energy as your intention, remember your Angel Message for today:

loving others in their own chosen path is setting the energy you want in your world.

The Gabriel Messages #11

The prayers you offer for others are a ticket to Higher Consciousness, because the gifts and blessings sent out in Light and Love have a ten-fold return.

Dear One,

Sometimes it feels as though prayer is the only thing you can do for another person, and you wish you could do more. Prayer is, however, the greatest gift you can give.

When you pray for another, you are sending a blessing of love and increased light-filled energy. This can bring them an expanded perspective on their life, an awareness of a Greater Power working within them as love. They may not know why they feel better, they just know they do. God's love is the power that can heal all things. All you have to do in prayer is ask that another to be filled with this Divine Love and a perfect outflow of energy from a Higher Source will occur.

Prayer is often the last thing one thinks about when situations become disturbing. In truth, prayer is most helpful as the first and not the last resort. You may not know what is best for another, but their Higher Power does. Each person has a guardian Angel ready to respond to the prayers offered for another. It is very simple just to pray that the Angels bless someone and lead them to their highest good. Praying for such divine outworking has tremendous potential and power. It opens the door to the place where miracles occur.

When you pray for a miracle in any situation, you are letting the Universe know that you are willing to receive it. A conscious opening occurs. Ways are revealed which have not been previously thought of. It is the natural order to have miraculous occurrences in life. Your awareness of this truth increases your faith and belief in Divine Solutions. This belief is what opens the door.

Your faith is the healing elixir in all situations and prayer sets it all in motion.

All that is released to Divine Spirit, with the intention of perfect outworking for the highest good of all concerned, is blessed. This blessing increases the return of energy to the person offering the prayer. There is no real way to measure the energy of God's return blessings, but ten times seems to be something the mind can accept. However, prayers offered only with the thought of tenfold return do not carry the powerful intention of a miraculous outworking. A pure release to Divine Will is necessary, with the intent to allow a greater power to work through each person and each situation. This is the way to create miracles.

Prayer is a simple thought, a blessing given freely. It needs no special place, time or words. Your heart carries this spiritual energy, and has the intention for good. This is all you need to bring blessings to the life of another and into your world. As a bonus you are blessed also. This is a universal gift to you for desiring good in your world and in the lives of others. It is the Grace of God. Receive it freely, with gratitude.

Remember your message from the Angels today:

the prayers you offer for others are a ticket to Higher Consciousness, because the gifts and blessings sent out in Light and Love have a ten fold return.

The Gabriel Messages #12

There is never a time when you are not wrapped in the wings of Pure Love.

Dear One,

This is a time when the forces of light and love are very close to your daily consciousness and you are blessed in a way you have never before known. You have only to turn your attention away from what does not work in your life, and turn towards that which is positive and worthwhile. This may sound simplistic and too good to be true, especially when you have such overwhelming problems in your world today. However, you are not alone. In fact there is never a time when you are not wrapped in the wings of pure love.

Turn your attention to the feeling of love that is hovering around you. With a little imagination you can even feel the presence of the angelic beings who are working closely with your earth at this time. The Angels carry a vibration very different from your normal world. It is a powerful force of love and light. Imagine being enfolded in this light, with an incredible sense of Divine Love flowing into your heart. Let this love spread throughout your entire body. As this love fills you and surrounds you, your fears begin to drop away, and beauty becomes a greater part of your life.

Practice

Imagine what it would feel like to be filled with so much beauty and love that it would not matter where you were, or what your physical eyes could see at any moment. You would be basking in the warmth and goodness of the loving presence of the Angels and this would transform your perception of reality. When you can continue to remember that you are wrapped in wings of pure love, and that you are filled with loving light, you will begin to vibrate at a higher level of consciousness and this in turn will create change in your immediate world, on a physical level. Just this small shift in your awareness can create miracles.

To have a "miracle" consciousness is to have the awareness that this is your true state of being. To be in that miraculous glow of love, to trust in the universal flow of your life and to receive a new level of goodness – this is the way you were meant to live. In order to actually live this way, however, you must turn the focus of your attention away from problems and troubles toward the essence of Spirit within all things. Sometimes this means that you must close your physical eyes and really feel the wings of pure love surrounding you. So take time everyday to turn within yourself, to the presence of God and the Angels. Where your attention goes, energy flows. Ask yourself if you are giving more attention to the challenges of your world or to your miraculous link with the Universal Power of good that exists in all things.

You are not alone. You have powerful forces available to you in order to begin this transformational work in your life. You have a guardian Angel whose job it is to assist you, and you have the benevolent Spirit that is the energy within all things. These gifts exist within you, and within all situations occurring in your life. At times it may be difficult to see the gift in your present situation. But there is a gift, and asking to see it will help to bring this awareness to your consciousness.

So as you go through your day, keep remembering that you are incredibly loved. Not only by the Divine Presence within all things, but the Angels are with you, blessing you in every moment. Remember also:

there is never a time when you are not wrapped in wings of Pure Love.

The Gabriel Messages #13

The Inner Spirit working outward in your life is the only place where stability can be found in these changing times.

Dear One,

You have found that your world is speeding up, even a sense of frantic activity without a sense of accomplishment. You have found yourself searching for meaning in all that you are doing when it does not feel like enough.

The truth is that there is an increase in the energy of the earth's vibrational field. Because of this, people are experiencing a shift in consciousness that encourages their search for meaning in all that they do. And Universal Consciousness is now more easily available to all who seek than ever before. This increase in energy is also creating great and rapid change in the world around you. Information is more available, tremendous earth changes, such as earthquakes, fires and hurricanes, seem to be occurring with more frequency, and the very fabric of social, political and family life seems to have shifted into unknown areas. All these occurrences are in the world of appearance, the world outside yourself. They point out the fact that you can no longer look to your outside world to bring you a sense of stability. You must come back to yourself and find that still point of peace, harmony and wisdom within. This is the only place of stability in these changing times.

Within you there is a place of such peace that you can totally relax there and allow it to permeate your being. Within you is found the truth and joy and meaning which you have sought in vain from the world outside yourself. Come now and allow yourself to experience this place within, where you can be free just to be. It is as close as your breath. And it is with your breath, and the power of your thoughts and imagination, that you can begin to experience your Higher Self and your connection to the Divine.

Practice

Take a few deep and centering breaths. Bring your attention to the place just below your navel, and imagine that you have found yourself in a very peaceful garden. You can make this garden the most beautiful place you have ever seen. Create flowing brooks and peaceful ponds, flowers and shady trees. Make it a place that you will long to come back to again and again. Allow yourself to relax and absorb the peace and beauty of this garden. Give yourself time to meet with your guardian Angel and with your Higher Self to receive all the wisdom, guidance and love that you need.

It may take a little practice to find this peaceful place within yourself, but it won't be long before, after only a few balanced breaths, you will be able to go there without effort. When you give yourself this time of quiet, you will notice that your outer world will not have the power to pull you away from this still place of peace. This is true stability. It is from this still point within that you will be able to live in this time of change and not feel alone or abandoned. You will be able to connect deeply with the support you need.

Like a wheel whose spokes appear to revolve very quickly, but whose center has quiet movement connecting all the links around it, this revolution of stillness within you will transform your outer world into one of harmony, love and peace.

Remember to ask for this stillness. Ask for the experience of a peaceful garden. Ask for your personal connection to the Source of all life. It all begins with you, with your thoughts, and with the balanced breath that is your connecting link. It is all there for you if you but give yourself the time.

Remember your message from the Angels today:

the Inner Spirit working outward in your life in the only place where stability can be found in these changing times.

The Gabriel Messages #14

Do not allow yourself to dwell in past patterns. Simply accept those choices and move ahead.

Dear One,

As you move through your life you are given many opportunities for growth. There may have been times when you chose ways of behavior which now seem inappropriate, and may even cause you great pain when you think of them. You may also have a sense of guilt for the pain you feel you caused others. You are here at this place and time, reading these words, to know that it is time to accept the choices you made in the past and to move on with your life.

What occurred in the past is over. To continue to beat yourself up or wish you had done things differently serves no purpose. There comes a time for forgiveness, and this is what is necessary before you can make the changes you want for your future. When you continue to relive past experiences, it keeps you dwelling in those patterns of behavior, even if you are no longer acting them out. It is necessary to clear those patterns through compassion and forgiveness.

Forgiveness is love in action. It is a cleansing balm that can soothe the tattered places of your mind. There is no person on earth who, as a child of God, does not deserve forgiveness. All that you have been through and all the actions you have taken up to this moment, have taught you lessons you have needed to learn. This is true for everyone. You will continue to receive the same lessons over and over, even if there is a slight variation in the form, until you do learn them.

It is helpful to remember your life is a huge school, where learning experiences are given in every moment to bring you to the peace and light of the Divine Presence within you. At a certain point in life, the peace of God is more important than anything else. All the choices you make will be made from the inner awareness: "does this bring me closer to peace?" It is helpful to pray for others that they too might also find this place of peace within themselves.

Joy is found in total forgiveness. It can free you to live your life in the present moment because you will no longer be looking back at what occurred in the past, or worrying about the future. When you find yourself living wholly in the moment, an energy is released within you. You can find passion for living, and a connection to the Source of all your good. From this place, all the decisions you make and the actions you take will be for the highest good of all concerned. From this place you can find the peace you have been searching for. It is in this moment right now, and it is within you.

Practice

Take the time to look at what is worrying you or what things in your life cause you pain when you remember them. It can be helpful to make a list, or write a letter to God or to the Angels and say all that you want to about that subject. Don't hold back. It's okay to go on and on, and repeat yourself. The important thing is that you clear your mind and emotions.

It may be helpful to picture yourself as a small child who did something which was not appropriate. Forgive this child of God, for if you had known how to do it differently, you would have. This is true for others involved in any situation. Forgive their inner child, even if you cannot forgive their actions.

When you feel complete, sit quietly and breathe balanced breaths. Call on the Angels of Light and Love to be with you and guide your way. Next, pray to your Higher Power, and ask for forgiveness for those actions that may still cause you pain. Ask that you might feel God's forgiveness at the deepest level of your being.

Have an intention to heal all experiences within you from the past so you may now live in peace. When you have this intention, the flow of energy in your life will move in the way that will reflect your highest good. In this truth you can trust. Free yourself by forgiving the past, accepting the present moment as it is, and allowing miracles to be your future.

This is as it shall be when you remember your inspiration for today:

do not dwell in past patterns. Simply accept those choices and move ahead.

The Gabriel Messages #15

Be grateful for all that you have and all that you are.

Dear One,

You have so much to be grateful for. At times it may feel as though life is hard, and yet if you can pull back from its drama, you will see how fortunate you truly are. Even the lessons you are now going through are a blessing.

Though it may feel as if you don't have enough – whether it's time, money, health, or love – you actually have been blessed with a tremendous gift. That gift is your life. A physical body is a wondrous blessing. Take time to observe the miraculous occurrences in your body. It is a miracle that messages are transmitted from your brain so there is movement in different parts of your body. It is a miracle that you don't have to tell your heart to beat or your stomach to digest. The physical body is a constant source of awe when you consider it a gift from God. You are to use this body to learn your lessons in life and to help bring heaven to earth. You are here to create a better world for all. You are here to learn to find peace and harmony within yourself so all people on earth may experience this. One person finding inner peace helps to bring peace to the entire world.

You are a part of a wondrous Presence in whom you live, move and have your being. The presence of Spirit exists beneath all your tumultuous thoughts, and between your breaths. You are here to remember this fact, and to live in this awareness at all times. This Presence is constantly giving, and you can consistently receive the blessings available by focusing your attention on the truth of who you are. You can know that whatever situation is occurring in your life, or in the world, God is in the midst of it all.

Practice

Be grateful for this gift of Universal Presence within you. Be grateful for your body and for the lessons you are learning which assist your spiritual progress. Take the time to see the beauty in nature – a flower, tree or bird, and be grateful for the beauty of the Divine there and within all things.

Be grateful for the presence of the Angels in your life. These messengers from God are a powerful force for love and wisdom in your world. You can call upon them at any moment, and their assistance is available to you. This is a supreme gift.

And be grateful for all that you are. You are a spark of light radiating God's Presence on the earth. You are God's Love expressing to others. You are God's Wisdom remembering the truth of Divine Order in every situation. You

are so much more than what you seem. Remember the expansiveness of your true nature, and be grateful.

Your gratitude opens the floodgates for Heaven's blessings. Gratitude creates an energy that beckons good into your life. When you are grateful, you feel more peaceful and more fulfilled. It is easier to remember that God is within all people and situations. And you can begin to be a witness rather than being embroiled in life's dramas. You hold the key to peace on earth. As you gratefully focus on the truth of your divine nature, remember your message from the Angels today:

be grateful for all that you have and all that you are.

The Gabriel Messages #16

Be aware that the answers to all you are seeking are within you.

Dear One,

Seeking answers to your life's questions outside yourself will seldom be necessary. This may seem impossible to you and yet we are now in a time when people no longer need an intermediary with God, the Source of all Life.

There has been a quickening in the electrical energy on and around planet earth. Because you are an electrical being you are very much affected by this increased energy-frequency. A higher level of energy enables you to attune yourself to a finer vibration, which allows you to consciously receive the resonance of wisdom and love from the Divine Mind. Wisdom and love come through your energy field as light energy, which carries with it information allowing you to live more in harmony with the needs of your soul.

This means that as you pray and meditate, you draw to yourself, like a magnet, a high frequency of light and love-filled energy. As this energy permeates your being it opens your mind to receive answers to any questions you put forth. You have the capacity to be a conduit for information, as well as for the ecstasy of God's love.

It may not seem possible to receive answers to complicated questions. Yet this is true only when fear and doubt cloud your perception. Pray to receive clearly, and pray to know the truth that is in your highest good. You can ask to know beyond a shadow of a doubt. Then you can follow the "Diamond Covenant of Moses." This declares that you are willing to do whatever is revealed to you, when you know beyond a shadow of a doubt that which is in your highest good. This willingness to follow your inner guidance sets up a flow of energy through you, which allows your Higher Self to be attuned to your conscious mind.

When you are in a relaxed and expanded state of being, you have access to all the wisdom of the universe. The Angels are available to flood your mind with love and light if you ask. When your being is filled with love and light, you understand consciously what steps to take in any situation. This inner knowing may not be immediately apparent to your conscious mind. However as you go about your day, you will begin to respond to all situations with greater calm and certainty. When you look back, you will see how you just "knew" what to do.

Practice

Try writing your question on a piece of paper. Have it with a pen close to you as you meditate, and pray to know the truth beyond a shadow of a doubt. Call on your personal Angelic teacher. Ask that your higher self be in tune with Divine Mind. Now sit, breathe in a rhythmic way and allow your mind and body to relax. Visualize yourself sitting in a pillar of light connecting Heaven and Earth. After sufficient uninterrupted time, you may feel the impulse to write.

While you pray and meditate you are in an expanded consciousness. From this place all answers are obvious, yet the critical nature of the mind loves to make judgments. Do not read your answer right away. This will defuse your inner critic. After an hour or so, go back and read what you have written. Most likely you will surprise yourself with the simple, practical solutions to your questions. With practice this process becomes easier, as you set up a direct conduit to your higher self, that part of you in touch with the angelic dimensions and divine guidance.

This is the dawning age of direct guidance and wisdom. You no longer need priests, gurus or those outside yourself to show you what is in your highest good. This does not mean that teachers and role models are not important. It does mean that you do not have to seek outside yourself to find the answers to your most important questions. No one else knows more than you what is right for your life. When you are aligned with God and spend quiet time in prayer and meditation, all that you want to know will be there for you.

Be aware that the answers to all you are seeking are within you.

The Gabriel Messages #17

True Wisdom and Pure Love go hand in hand. You must love all of yourself before Pure Wisdom takes solid root within you.

Dear One,

When you receive pure love from your Divine Source and offer it to yourself, your life will transform. Loving yourself means that you accept yourself as a student of life. You know that you are growing every day, and deep within is the spark of enlightened consciousness that is God. Focusing on this place of light will assist it to grow. When the light of Divine love grows it enlightens your mind and heart, so you see your life from a more expanded perspective. This allows you to tap into the graceful flow of the universe and to live in more peace and harmony. Loving yourself includes being able to see the tricks of ego and the aspects of your personality that could be improved. After you see clearly, bless these parts of yourself. This blessing energy will allow the love of God to flow through you.

Your fears will drop away, and you will operate from a loving heart in every moment.

If self-criticism created perfection, you would be perfect by now. It doesn't work that way so be kind to yourself. You are in a human body on the earth plane to gain an education. Your soul's growth is in the direction of perfection, but it's a process.

You are like a lump of coal becoming a diamond. It does no good to hate the rough form and wish it were a diamond. What it takes is a step-by-step process, with the proper tools, applied with diligence and care. Recognize your incredible potential to be a diamond. Allow the Angels to assist the process of sanding your rough edges. Know it takes some time and love yourself for caring enough about your world that you want to be the best you can be.

Be as patient and caring with yourself as you would with a little child. Hold fast to the light of God within you. Ask for assistance from the Angels and trust the process. You are becoming stronger and more beautiful every day. Know you are incredibly loved and you deserve all the good life has to offer.

Remember:

true Wisdom and Pure Love go hand in hand. You must love all of yourself before Pure Wisdom takes solid root within you.

The Gabriel Messages #18

Ask to be a receptacle for pure Light, then allow the empty chalice within to drink in the sweetness which is God's Love.

Dear One,

When you ask to be a receptacle for pure light, you are saying that you have space within you, and that you are willing to fill this space with love and all that which is God. You are saying that you want to be filled with Spirit, and assist the process of bringing Heaven to Earth.

This is important work for everyone, and it does not interfere with other work or with family life. Recognize that your purpose on this planet is to be a bridge between Heaven and Earth, so that all beings may live in greater harmony, peace and love. This mission requires assistance from all. Each person who turns toward the light assists this purpose and raises the collective consciousness of the planet. The way to bring peace on earth is through one person at a time. So always believe there is much you can do.

Being a receptacle for pure light expands your mind and creates new ways of responding to situations in your life. Being a receptacle for pure light also means you are in prayer for yourself and others. Whenever you pray you open the door for more light to come through you. Prayer is a great form of purification, and raises the vibration of self and others. The higher the vibration, the more peace and love one will feel.

Practice

Visualization can greatly assist the process of being a holy vessel. Give yourself time to sit quietly, away from the world. Flowers and candles can uplift the energy around you and help you feel more expansive. Take some time to breathe balanced breaths, until you are in a calm and relaxed state. Ask God that you may be a receptacle for pure light and then imagine that your body is a beautiful golden chalice. See it empty, or only partially filled with light. Imagine that you are sitting under a waterfall of God's golden light. This golden light has great power and contains both wisdom and love. Imagine that you are drinking this sweet light, and as it fills up your golden chalice, you are absorbing love and wisdom into every fiber of your being. The more full that your vessel becomes, the more loving and blissful you feel. Make your chalice very large, so your entire energy field is expanded.

Take time every day to sit in this light and love. Drink in this light, then let it shine into the world, so all may know the truth of God's presence. You will find yourself becoming more loving, patient and clear. Decisions will be easier as you feel connected to a greater Source of wisdom within.

This simple exercise holds great power, and whenever or wherever it is done, it will allow you to be attuned to your God Source at all times. The more often you do it, the stronger you will become. The greater the level of strength, light and love you are able to hold within you, the easier it will be to serve God and to assist others. You will be one who is a bridge between Heaven and Earth when you remember your inspiration for today:

ask to be a receptacle for pure Light, then allow the empty chalice within you to drink in the sweetness which is God's Love.

The Gabriel Messages #19

Without patience you can never understand the meaning of Divine Timing.

Dear One,

Your presence in the world in a conscious manner leads to the opening of the consciousness of all people. Your task is to carry the light of love and truth with you wherever you go, no matter what you are doing. Through this intention you will bring more peace and light into the world.

Being a visionary, you see in your mind that which you wish to accomplish. It becomes your intention, as if you are taking aim, pulling back the bow and shooting your arrow toward your target. With this clarity, you will surely reach your mark. There is, however, the question of when.

At work in the world is the principle of Divine Timing. It is one of the immutable laws in the universe, such as Divine Order and Divine Justice. It is not something that you can push to make it go faster. There are times when you must wait upon the will of God in order to have your dream manifest in the most appropriate way for the highest good. This requires patience. It is sometimes difficult to have patience when you can see your vision so clearly. Often there is the desire to make it happen now. This is not God's will but the ego's will at work. You might be able to force the manifestation of certain parts of your vision, but it will not feel right once this occurs. It will feel as though you are pushing the river. When all is flowing according to God's will, miracles occur. You can ride the wave of this energy and it feels effortless.

Practice

Imagine that you are at one of those points in your life when you want very badly to have a certain vision manifest. Let's say you really want it now but you are struggling against a wall of obstacles. If you are mentally or emotionally tense, anxious and impatient, anything that you do physically at this time will be pushing at the energy already at work. It is at these times that you must step aside, even though it may be most difficult. Release your striving, and turn the whole situation over to God and the Angels.

You can assist the manifestation of your dream by simply sitting quietly and breathing in the light of truth and wisdom. As you continue to breathe these balanced breaths, see yourself in a pillar of golden light. This is the light of peace, love and wisdom that connects you with Divine Inspiration and the nurturing presence of the earth. While sitting in this light, in your mind's eye remember your vision, the dream that you want for your life at this time. Allow your dream to be energized by this pillar of golden light. Know in your heart that you always receive that which is in your highest good. Know that the Angels are blessing you with love and wisdom. They are blessing all that you need to do in order to have your dream. Feel this loving presence with you, enfolding you in love and light. Feel peace permeating every fiber of your being. Know in your heart that all will come to you in perfect divine timing. Give thanks for all the blessings in your life. Give thanks that this dream is manifesting in its own perfect and right time for your highest good. And as you exhale, release this vision to God and the Angels and allow this energy to work for you.

This practice will help give you patience and trust in Divine Timing. With a small amount of conscious effort you can begin to apply these principles to your day to day living and create a life filled with more peace, joy and love. This is the God's will for all. Call on the Angels for assistance and remember to take time to breathe and receive the knowing in your heart that all is in the flow of Divine Will.

Remember your message for today:

without patience you can never understand the meaning of Divine Timing.

The Gabriel Messages #20

Release any need to cling to the status quo. You are being asked to let go into the power of Light, which will allow you to live in your Truth.

Dear One,

It is a new time. It is a new moment. When you cling to the status quo, you are clinging to the way things used to be. Sometimes it feels safer to hold to the old way. Change can be frightening and, yet, is your world not changing constantly? In holding on to the status quo, you are clinging to a thought of how something used to be, when you have the power to change it for the better this very moment.

There is tremendous power in your thoughts. A thought is like a prayer to the universe, asking for what you want. If your thoughts are unconscious, if fears play a large part in what goes on in your mind, in effect you are asking for the things that frighten you to come into your life.

Fear is part of the status quo and the greatest fear seems to be of the unknown. Yet it is not possible to always know exactly what is to be. You are being asked to let go of your fears and allow the power of Divine Light to guide, nourish and protect you.

Letting go is a moment to moment process. It is surrendering to the flow of life. Let go into the light, which is the flow of God moving within you at every moment. The Divine Presence is the only constant in the midst of change. This is a truth you can trust. Is not the power of light and love a greater attraction than fear and doubt? It is your attachment to wanting things never to change that holds you back.

Simply ask clearly for what you want from the Higher Power and the Angels. All the assistance you need is available to you, if you but ask. When you are free from old fears and attachments, you will know the freedom and joy of your truth. Your truth is always what makes you happy, and this is Divine Will for you at all times – God wants you to be happy.

Pray to live in the light of your truth. Know that you are divinely guided at all times. Ask for assistance to let go of fears that no longer serve you. Allow the grace of the Angels to work through you knowing you are profoundly loved.

Remember:

release any need to cling to the status quo. You are being asked to let go into the power of Light, which will allow you to live in your Truth.

The Gabriel Messages #21

Be aware of the simple truth that God exists in all circumstances.

Dear One,

The light of God is always shining. This light exists in all people, all things and all circumstances. Awareness of this light will bring it into your consciousness, enabling you to see from an enlightened perspective.

The Divine Presence is the very energy in which we live, move and have our being. This energy is infinite and all-encompassing and exists in all situations. This truth may be difficult to remember at times. In fact, it may appear as though there is nothing but darkness. However, remembering this Divine Power will bring light into every dark circumstance.

Energy follows thought. If you think of God in any situation, the very thought produces illumination, as though a candle were lit in a dark room. When you ask for divine outworking, that prayer directs this divine energy so that you will be surrounded with heavenly light and spiritual good will flow through your entire being.

Awareness of Divine Light enlightens every situation. Each time we turn toward the Source of true light we are blessed. When even one person turns toward the light of God, the earth is blessed. This blessing creates change. At times this change can be instantaneous, at other times healing can occur in a less obvious way. Have faith, and know healing happens in accordance with divine timing. Always affirm the greater truth in every situation in order to bring your awareness back to the Divine Presence.

When you call upon your guardian Angel, you focus upon the light in the midst of your darkness. Your guardian Angel, and all Angelic messengers from God are here to assist you in bringing more light and love into your life. No matter what it looks like, no matter how dire the circumstances may appear to be, you will receive immediate assistance when you call on the Angels for help. Ask for what you truly want in your life. Do your best *not* to focus on how bad things seem to be, but turn your attention toward the light, and you will indeed find the situation enlightened.

By being aware of the simple truth that God exists in all situations, you can bring light into your life. Turning your attention toward Heaven by the use of your breath can change the very energy in your world. Remember to create a cocoon of protective, nurturing light around you by giving yourself time to breathe balanced breaths and to pray for the qualities you want to see manifest in your life.

Where your focus goes, energy flows. The question is: do you want to dwell in darkness or in light? It is your choice. Return through your breath to this cocoon of golden light. You will come to the place where you are safe, surrounded and filled with God's love at all times. Your world will begin to change when you turn your attention to this loving presence of divine everlasting light.

This may all seem too easy. However we will ask you to remember that your message from the Angels today is:

be aware of the simple truth that God exists in all circumstances

The Gabriel Messages #22

Call on us often and picture the wings of Angels enfolding you in Light.

Dear One,

To call on the Angels does not symbolize weakness, it shows strength. It takes great courage to ask for assistance. There is a thought-form in your society that says you must "do it alone" if you are to be considered responsible and mature. This, however, creates a great burden for you in your world because there is so much to deal with in worldly life. It is not easy to live in an earth body, so assistance is necessary in order to live in a happier, more harmonious way.

You cannot look for answers to life's challenges in the world around you. The answers and the way are in the light of truth and wisdom. This is the light of God's love and it is the comfort offered by the Angels. When you ask for assistance, light and love flow to you immediately. This expands your conscious awareness so you can see the greater truth in any situation. This gives you freedom to act in ways that you know are in your highest good.

You are provided with guardian Angels that are with you throughout your life. They are always available for you to call upon, to ask questions of, and to provide the depth of companionship for which your soul longs. Human companions are not capable of giving you the depth, wisdom, and strength that the Angels can give you.

If this level of relationship is something you desire, call on your Angelic friends now. There has never been a time when the Angels were so closely available as they are at this time. Presently, the veils are very thin between the worlds. This means that you can pray and take the time to call in the presence of your guardian Angels and they will be there for you. You can ask for signs of proof. You can ask to bask in their loving light. All this will occur. But your desire for a personal relationship is necessary to bring the Angels into your conscious awareness. This is easy for you to do. Use the power of your imagination and allow your mind to soar in expansive ways.

Release now the burden of having to do it alone. Call on the Angels often. Ask for help in every situation. You will be held in comforting wings of loving light and your way will be cleared.

This is an Angelic promise to you. We love you and bless you always. Remember:

call on us often and picture the wings of Angels enfolding you in Light.

The Gabriel Messages #23

All the money I give is blessed and returned to me multiplied.

Dear One,

You have been given limitless resources to use in your earth life. These limitless resources include wondrous beauty, relationships that affirm the divinity within you, freedom to be the best you can be, and an abundant flow of money. This flow of money is sometimes the most difficult of God's gifts for you to see in your life. You stand in the midst of this energy, which can be used to make your life more comfortable, and yet many times, your ability to receive these resources is limited by your thoughts and by your resistance to receiving.

This energy from the Divine Source, which is called money, has the same properties inherent in it that any of God's gifts have, such as love and joy. It is the strong energy of Life Force, which you can tap into, in order to receive the blessings of abundant cash flow.

One easy way to make yourself more available to money is by creating thoughts of unlimited resources in your mind. Your thoughts create your reality. When you entertain thoughts of lack, of "not enough" in your life, this translates in your world as not enough money to meet your needs. There must be a shift in your thinking before you can attract an abundant level of income to yourself. One way to change your consciousness is by affirmations. We have given you a very powerful affirmation to say every day, and especially every time you write checks or spend money, even if it is only pennies. This affirmation is:

all the money I give is blessed and returned to me multiplied.

When you bless anything – your friends, children, life partners, jobs, etc. – the inherent good within is increased. Blessing leads to an increase in energy. So when you bless all the money you spend, you increase the energy it carries into the world.

You have heard the expression, what goes around, comes around. This is a basic principle: what you give is what you receive. When you give blessings, you receive blessings. When you give out of fear of lack, you receive back what you fear – lack of abundant income. Fear is a very powerful force that can attract to you what you fear most. Love and blessings are even more powerful and can bring to you that which is blessed with love. Remember that God is the source of your supply and there are no shortages. This inexhaustible resource of Spirit is equal to every need you may have.

Many people come to the Ocean of Abundance with only a teaspoon when they could bring a bucket or a much larger vessel. You can consciously choose to expand your ability to receive and to enlarge your own container. One way to do this is through prayers of gratitude and blessings for what you already have and for what you will receive. These prayers will help to lift your consciousness and bring you to a place where you can affirm the truth that you are one with abundant life and with the abundant flow of money and prosperity in the world. Blessing all the money you give is another way to do this.

God's abundance exists everywhere, and you can move into the stream of consciousness that allows you to have all your needs met, when you develop the attitude of gratitude, blessing, and affirming the Divine Truth of abundance within all things. So begin now to bless that which you have and bless those you love. Lift yourself up so you can begin to see that which is good in your life. And remember your message from the Angels today:

all the money I give is blessed and returned to me multiplied.

The Gabriel Messages #24

You attract to you only that which is in your consciousness.

Dear One,

Your thoughts are magnetic. Even when you are not conscious of what you are thinking, the power of your thoughts affects your life. What you hold in your mind creates a level of consciousness, and this influences that which you experience in your world. So, if you want to change the world you live in, start with your own thoughts and feelings.

There are many levels of consciousness. Total consciousness can be called oneness with the Mind of God. This is the place where the master teachers dwell, and it is a level of awareness that, ultimately, all humans seek to attain. The closer you come to submersion in this Divine Presence, the greater a force for good you are on the planet.

Praying for attainment of conscious union with God will increase the level of energy you work with in daily life, generating a high vibrational frequency within your mind, and thus encouraging more positive thinking at all times. Positive thoughts, when held in conscious awareness, can affect everyone around you in a positive way as well. Thoughts are "catching." As all minds are a part of the Mind of God, the minds of all people are linked. Through this link you can spread thoughts of darkness and fear or thoughts of love and forgiveness. It is your choice, and it takes moment to moment awareness.

Sometimes it doesn't seem like you have a choice about the way you are feeling. Yet, whether this darkness is coming from you, or you are being affected by the consciousness of people around you, it is up to you to do what you can to change your thoughts. If you don't, a downward spiral of energy is created, and more effort is necessary to come back to a loving perspective.

Practice

There are some very simple exercises that can be used to shift these thoughts and feelings. First, accept that your thoughts are causing you to suffer. Next, just be willing to change.

Your intention to create change will set that energy into motion. When you know what qualities you want in your world, you create that intention in your consciousness. For instance, is it your intention to live in peace, love and harmony? Or is it your intent to live in struggle, fear or intolerance? When you choose to live in the greater energy frequency of love and acceptance, the universe rejoices and all manner of assistance becomes instantly available to you.

Setting your intention is really a form of prayer, because it is stating what you want to the Universe. You can ask for specific qualities, and also for assistance in receiving them. It matters not to Whom you pray. There is only one God, whose power is available to you when you ask, and when you surrender your personal will to the greater Divine Will.

Changing your world starts within you, in your thoughts and feelings. Hold in your conscious awareness only that which you want to experience throughout your day. You will find yourself attracting more love, harmony and divine order to every area of your life and you will lift not only your own consciousness, but that of the world. Know that the Angels are guiding and blessing you so that all may be transformed, when you remember:

you attract to you only that which is in your consciousness.

The Gabriel Messages #25

Strengthen your conscious awareness of other states beyond the physical, communicate deeply within your self and learn to trust in your own answers.

Dear One,

You are here on this planet to develop yourself fully. When the ancient philosophers stated "Know Thyself," they were talking about the power of Self-awareness. This means not just one's consciousness of the physical, or even of the mental and emotional selves. To truly know oneself means a real discernment of your self as a multi-dimensional being.

You have the power within you to know planes of reality beyond the three-dimensional world in which you live. In fact, developing an awareness of these other states creates a link to the joy and love so many are seeking. These qualities you truly desire in life are beyond the physical plane. They exist in the expanded state of consciousness that is your bond with God, the Source of your very being. To commune within your self is to find these qualities. It requires a willingness to see beyond your outer self, and to take the time necessary to create a conscious awareness of the love and light within you.

Practice

As you sit quietly and breathe balanced breaths deeply and slowly, there are immediate results in mind, body and spirit. Imagine that you are sitting in a pillar of golden light joining Heaven to Earth through you. This allows you to enlarge your consciousness. When you add prayer asking for what you want in your life, you allow the grace of the Angels to work for you.

On this free-will plane of existence you need to ask for their assistance or they will not interfere. This does not necessarily mean a formal prayer. Asking can be as simple as saying the words for the qualities you want in your life, such as love, peace and harmony. Meditating on these qualities can literally change your life and create a more abundant, joy-filled existence. It allows you to tap into your Higher Self and your guardian Angels, so you are communicating with the deepest levels of your being.

From this place, the answers you receive will be from a level of Divine Order, and all that follows will be for the highest good of all concerned. You will receive intuition and know the actions and words that will best assist you with the challenges you face. Once you begin to act on your intuitive guidance, you will start to trust your self. Life will feel easier. You won't need to continue looking to others for the answers. With every fiber of your being you will know what is truth in your life.

Trusting in your self does not mean you are alone, for you are never alone. At all times, you have with you Angels to assist you. Some have been with you for eons of time. Working in harmony with the Light of God, they know you at the deepest level of your soul. It is comforting to know that you are always wrapped in their wings of pure love and cared for beyond your capacity to understand.

It is this link within the self that most people are seeking. They hunger for knowledge of the love that is within them. It is readily available through prayer and taking time to sit and breathe in light and love in a conscious manner. So give your self the gift of sitting in light and love every day for five minutes. It is a simple thing that will provide you with wondrous joy.

The Angels are ready now to lead you into the light of your true Self. Create a conscious relationship with your Higher Power and find the joy you so desire to have. Ask for assistance from the Angels. Begin to do this every day and miracles will surely occur, for miracles are your birthright and the natural state of your being. Know that you deserve to have your life filled with Love, Joy and Miracles. Learn to communicate within and trust in your own truth. This is the way you will live to your fullest potential and fulfill your highest destiny on earth.

We love you and bless you with all that is good. Remember your message from the Angels today:

strengthen your conscious awareness of other states beyond the physical, communicate deeply within yourself and learn to trust in your own answers.

The Gabriel Messages #26

Ground any excess energy such as fear, anxiety or anger into the earth and bring an open heart into the present moment.

Dear One,

Grounding excess energy means being aware that any time you are feeling anxious, angry, fearful or over-excited, you are experiencing excess energy in your body which can be consciously redirected. This energy is very potent and can be used in a constructive way.

A metaphor might be useful. In electrical terms, it is necessary to have something called the "ground." For instance, in a house there is a grounding wire which connects to the earth so electricity flows in the proper circuits. It is similar with your body as you are receiving energy from the Divine Source at all times. There are perfect channels in your body for the energy to flow through. If you are not grounded, that is, if you are so caught up in your mental activity that you are not consciously aware of your connection to the earth, this energy can flow into channels that may feel uncomfortable. It can then circulate through your nervous system, over-stimulating your mind and causing anxiety and other mental imbalances. When you notice yourself feeling upset and anxious, it is very helpful to remember that you have feet as well as a head.

Practice

Your feet are in touch with the earth, a place of bountiful supply and nourishing energy. When you are aware of the earth's presence, you feel supported and nurtured. You can visualize energy leaving your feet and moving in beams of light into the earth. This will allow the excess energy in your mind to dissipate.

It will also serve to calm your emotional body.

If you have mountains, trees or ocean near you, it can be useful to see these as places to ground excess energy. You can visualize light beams radiating from your feet, or pillars of light from heaven to earth, or whatever image suits you. This is a very simple but powerful tool for you to use.

As you become more aware of this grounding process, you will begin to be more present in the moment. Being present means bringing an open heart to whatever situation is challenging you at the time. When your heart is open you are able to make decisions from a place of love and not fear. As more people do this, the consciousness of the whole planet is raised, as all minds are connected to the One Mind. All are blessed and can live more freely in love and peace.

You can be a part of this peace-filled evolution with the choices you make every day. Choose to live in love, not fear. Notice when you are running anxiety or anger through your body and are feeling "over-amped." Take the time to send this excess energy into the earth with a prayer asking to experience only love. Know that all on earth are blessed when one person chooses to open his or her heart in love to another. Know the earth is blessed when you give energy to her, so in turn, all will be blessed as this great planet gives back in sustenance and life. In these simple ways you can bring peace to the world when you...

ground any excess energy such as fear, anxiety or anger into the earth and bring an open heart into the present situation.

The Gabriel Messages #27

*Your prayers are a beacon calling to you the
Light and Wisdom you seek.*

Dear One,

Just as a ship at sea can find the land it is seeking through the beacon light on shore, so is the power of your prayers. The guiding light of your prayers sets an intention for your life that leads the way to all you require for an abundant, healthy and joy-filled life. Prayer is an alignment with God's energy. It connects you to the abundant Source where all is provided. Prayer is not something you save until there is a dire need. Prayer is a way of aligning your thoughts to create the opening for miracles in your life.

When you pray you are sending out a powerful thought that acts like a beacon light. This thought not only attracts what you are asking for, it sets a pattern of energy for the highest good in your life. It increases your conscious awareness of the power of great possibilities. Prayer creates a shift in your attitude so you can be a magnet for your good.

Your prayer does not have to be an elaborate ritual. Simple words that work for you are the easiest way to attune yourself to God. Prayer acts as a reminder that there is a Higher Power available to assist you in every area of your life.

Practice

Knowing that an attitude of gratitude can lift your awareness, it is often helpful to begin your prayers by giving thanks for that which already exists in your life. Proclaiming Divine Order is another powerful prayer when you don't know what else to ask for. When Divine Order exists in your life, you live in harmony, love and abundant joy.

Sometimes God seems very far away and too vast to comprehend. At those times calling forth your guardian Angel is like calling on a friend, someone to talk to and pour out the deepest feelings in your heart. Know that it is all right for you to ask for what you want. The abundant resource of spirit is equal to every demand, and you deserve to be happy, and abundantly blessed. It is often helpful to know the qualities you desire to attract to you when you pray. If you are lonely and asking for a mate, know clearly what you want in a life companion. These qualities could include a deep heart connection, understanding and harmony. When you ask directly for the qualities behind the physical attributes, it allows for a greater opening in your consciousness so you can receive at a deeper level.

Visualization can also assist your prayers. Imagine that you are a lighthouse on a rocky shore, a beacon of light. Feel the expansiveness as your light reaches out into the world around you. Know that your light is attracting your good to you and that you are assisting others by your beacon. When you become this light in your thoughts, it expands your consciousness and prepares the way for you to receive even greater light. It creates a new level of calming faith within you. So let your light shine. You are meant to be this beacon of light shining forth into the world for all to see.

Each person has this ability to shine, because each person is a part of the light, love and wisdom which is God. When you recognize this power within you, it will create the energy for miracles to occur. Believe that all the good in the universe is available for you, just because you are a beloved child of the Creator of all that is.

As you shine your light into the world, know that you are not alone. The abundant energy of God is pouring into you to assist you in keeping your light strong. Know that the Angels are also available as companions on your path, ready to assist you when you ask. You are a magnet for your good when you remember:

your prayers are a beacon calling to you the Light and Wisdom you seek.

The Gabriel Messages #28

*There has never been a time when you were alone,
no matter how you felt.*

Dear One,

If you only knew how much you are loved and cared for, you would see your life in a different light. There are Angels who have been with you since your birth, and some from before your birth who have been with you for eons of time. These Angels are here to bless you, to protect you, to care for you and to love you as you walk your earthly journey.

You have only to turn within and you will find us. You have only to look around you, and you will find Angels manifested in different forms everywhere, giving love to you.

Open your mind and heart to receive this love and you will find miracles manifesting in your life. It is this willingness to receive that allows miracles to occur for you.

In your darkest hours we have been there. It is not that the Angels are here to take away your pain or your lessons learned through experience. The Angels are here for you to turn to in those hours of need. We are here to assist you so you will have the courage to go on, and find peace within your heart. You are on this planet to learn and to choose between the darkness and the light. Even if you choose darkness, there are Angels who will neither forsake you nor leave you. However, if you choose darkness you will *feel* very alone, and life will be a continuous struggle.

If you choose the light, the Angelic voices are raised in magnificent rejoicing and all manner of assistance, seen and unseen, will be there to illuminate your path. Choosing to live in the light can simply mean to turn over your burdens and struggles to a Higher Power, and to ask the Angels to assist you in finding your way to peace, happiness and prosperity. These are the qualities of God in which you are meant to live.

Choosing the light means praying for the Divine Presence to fill you to overflowing with love and peace. It means taking the time to visualize your self filled and surrounded by light, and even drinking in the light in order to nourish your heart and soul. Not only will this affect your mental and emotional state, but your physical body will also benefit.

The Angels are God's messengers. We live in Divine Light. All the forces of good in the universe are here to assist you so you too can live in the light and find peace and happiness within yourself. It is up to you to ask to know this as truth in your life. Open your mind and heart to receive all the love that is here for you right now. Remember your message from the Angels today:

There has never been a time when you were alone, no matter how you felt.

The Gabriel Messages #29

Bask in the wonder of life – go deep, soar high, follow your love and the joy of fulfillment is yours.

Dear One,

Life is a special gift from God, filled with infinite beauty. Your appreciation and gratitude for this beauty brings forth a new dimension of love within you. Take the time to pursue beauty. Find one flower and look with wondrous eyes upon this divine miracle. Notice the grace of a tree, the strength of its trunk, the power of the root system diving deep into the ground, and the play of the leaves in the sunlight. Put your arms around a tree and take a moment to sense the life force pulsing inside. This slow steady pulse will soothe and calm you in times of upset. Try sitting with your back against a tree and feel the peace grow within you. Listen to the songs of birds. They sing for the pure joy of it. This is nature in all its glory, and nature will always remind you of the beauty and wonder of Spirit.

Nature is one of the easiest ways to bask in the wonder of life. Just being aware of the miraculous occurrences in nature will stir the life force within you. There will be a reminder of times when you were a child and wonder lived at the forefront of your awareness. When you do this, your life takes on new meaning, a specialness.

Go deep within the feelings that connect you with Spirit. Be aware that you are a child of a benevolent Universe. Know that you are guided and protected by the Angels, and that who you are has great value to the world.

Soar high, and experience the incredible possibilities available to you at every moment. Anything is possible. Miracles are the natural state of being in the universe. Do not limit yourself by thinking you can't do what is important to you. Take the time to let your guardian Angel show you how you can accomplish all your dreams. In your meditation ask for this. You deserve to have that which makes you happy in your life.

Life is not meant to be a painful struggle without hope. Allowing new possibilities to play on the perimeters of your consciousness will begin the process of opening to full miracles. It is a process of allowing. It takes willingness to have your life be happier and more satisfying, even if you don't know how to do it. This willingness allows the forces of the universe to work for you. Allow yourself to open to miracles and to wondrous joy and gratitude for all that is available to you right now. Call on your Angelic presence to open the way to the miracles you deserve.

That is why we say:

bask in the wonder of life – go deep, soar high, follow your love and the joy of fulfillment will be yours.

The Gabriel Messages #30

Your way to freedom is by total acceptance of your incredible differences.

Dear One,

You have all been trained on this earth to fit in, to be a part of the way things are, to not go out of your way to change "what is." This is the training and yet, deep down most people know the truth – that it is only by being different that great changes can occur. Creativity lies in not being the same as everyone else. It results from listening and moving to a different tune – the one within, not outside, yourself.

So many people go through life feeling like an outcast, as if there is something wrong with them because they are different from other people. We are saying that these incredible differences are your gifts to give to the world. It is time to accept these differences and follow the lead of your creative self. Trying to fit in stifles your spirit. Freedom comes from knowing that those parts of you that are different from others hold the key to the joy and success that you desire.

It is in the acceptance of all of yourself that you will grow. You cannot love only that which you consider good and reject the other parts of yourself. Those other parts have purpose also. Understanding this will lead you to the place of wholeness that you long for. Wholeness means feeling total joy and love within yourself, feeling connection with your God Source and all of life. This is only possible if you can love and accept all the different parts of your personality and human make-up.

Self-criticism is one of the biggest factors in causing personal pain and slowing growth. So it would seem helpful to find a new role for your inner critic. There are many situations where this type of voice can be useful. Simply tell this side of your personality that you do appreciate its efforts to make you a better person, and keep it busy by sending it to work in those areas where you need more order and organization in your life. When you set judgment aside, you will begin to feel an expansiveness in your mind that allows inspiration and creativity to enter. You do have these creative parts of your personality. These are the parts of you that strive for expansion and are linked to your Higher Power and to the Angelic energy.

Practice

If you call upon the Angel of Inspiration and Creativity to show you ways to expand and enrich your life, a powerful focus of energy will begin to work in this direction. As you begin to use this new creative flow, it will become stronger and stronger. Creative Solutions will appear where they were not apparent previously. You will begin to break through old patterns of thought that hold you back, and doors will open to bring more joy, prosperity and originality into every area of your life.

When you can accept all parts of yourself as unique and special in their own way, there will be a sense of peace within you. There will be less fear in following your inner guidance and intuition. You will begin to trust yourself and to express your uniqueness. Remember that all the humans who are revered and considered great by the world, are highly valued for their differences from others, not for their sameness.

Keep this as your intention. Choose freedom and expansion instead of fear and contraction. Ask yourself what you would do if you could do anything. What would make your heart sing? Then ask for assistance from the Angels to create your vision for the good of all, and know all things are possible. Miracles are the natural order of the universe. Be willing to have things change in your life for the better. Be willing to see the good within you and accept the incredible differences that make you who you are. And always remember that you are greatly loved.

Your message from the Angels today is:

your way to freedom is by total acceptance of your incredible differences.

The Gabriel Messages #31

A full relationship with your Higher Self is possible when you give yourself time to receive Love from the deepest sources of your Being.

Dear One,

One of the most powerful and important relationships you have in this life is with your Higher Self. This is the part of you in full communion with God. Guidance and intuitive insight come from this place. There are several ways you can develop and strengthen this relationship between your personality awareness and your Higher Self, and all of them require patience, persistence and practice. One way is to learn to act on your intuition. How many times have you thought about doing something, ignored the thought, and then a situation arose when you said, "I knew I should have done that?" The more you listen to your inner voice and act on your intuition, the stronger this connection will become.

Another way to strengthen your connection to your Higher Self is through meditation. Meditation is a way of expanding your conscious awareness of states beyond your physical body. The physical world is the grossest level of manifestation and there are many planes of consciousness beyond it. Meditation is the key to reaching a deeper level of being, that still place within, where you are one with God.

Meditation is not difficult but it does require practice and persistence to attain a calm and focused mind. It may be frustrating at first, because the mind never seems to stop. Emotions and thoughts come up that clamor for attention. This is just the way thoughts work, so be patient and gently re-focus your mind on your breath as the object of your attention. It may be helpful to take the time to write out your feelings and thoughts before you meditate so that you can clear your mind more easily. Whatever you do to calm and clear yourself will be very helpful.

Practice

Sit quietly, breathe balanced breaths, and as you begin to feel more peaceful and centered, imagine a beautiful golden, healing light flowing around and through you,. There is incredible love within you, waiting only for your conscious permission to flood your entire being. Focus your attention on receiving the love of God. As you do, you will create a solid, conscious connection to your Higher Self. Allow yourself to bask in this love and let it permeate every cell of your being.

Create a beautiful place in your mind where you can go to sit in the silence that exists within you. Call on your angelic teachers for guidance and we will assist you in this process. The Angels are messengers of God, here to help you find peace, love and joy in your life. We can also assist your meditation process so you will find the love you need within yourself. Picture the Angels blessing you with wings of pure light, and we will be there. We love you and believe that you deserve to receive all that is good. When you take a little time every day to make your spiritual connection to God stronger, you will be amazed how your life will change. You will find guidance and wisdom available to you in a greater way than you ever imagined was possible. It takes only the willingness to give yourself time to breathe, focus and receive God's love.

Remember, your message from the Angels today:

a full relationship with your Higher Self is possible when you give yourself time to receive Love from the deepest sources of your Being.

The Gabriel Messages #32

When you connect deeply within to your enlightened state of mind, there is an expanded perception of the world you inhabit and any question can be answered.

Dear One,

You have within you an enlightened state of mind where Truth prevails and Divine Love surrounds you, filling all the dark places. Give yourself the gift of finding this place, and become so familiar with it that you are able to connect there with a breath and a thought.

This enlightened state within you is beyond normal waking consciousness and can even be called "super consciousness". It is the expanded place of light, peace and all wisdom. It is possible through prayer and meditation to connect deeply with this beautiful, expansive state within your mind.

It only takes a few minutes to sit quietly and breathe in light and love. When you do this and ask for guidance, you provide a fertile ground that can be planted with seeds of joy, peace and divine order in every area of your life. When you bring a question with you into your expanded place, the answer will become obvious. Even if it does not seem to be clear when you are sitting in your meditation place, it will "pop" into your mind as you go through your day if your intention to know the truth was strong.

Every day you can give yourself this gift and create a personal relationship with this enlightened state within you. From this place the Divine Mind is accessible and the Angels will inspire you. A state of peace will be the result. In this enlightened state of mind you can be filled with Divine Light and know all is well.

Remember your message from the Angels today:

when you connect deeply within to your enlightened state of mind, there is an expanded perception of the world, and any question can be answered.

The Gabriel Messages #33

Be willing to face the fears of the past and move into new dimensions of Love.

Dear One,

You have come to a time when you know that the way you have always perceived your world may seem like it is no longer working. It may even feel as though your childhood traumas or other things from your past you are not proud of, are crowding into your present awareness. This is a very good sign, because all memories come into your mind to be released, so that you can live in the present. We encourage this release of past memories and fear so you will be able to move on with your life. Whether you do this through prayer, personal journaling, talking to a friend or going through counseling, the important thing is to be willing to face the fears of the past, hold them in the light of loving awareness, and then let them go.

When the healing light of love, compassion and acceptance is shone on old patterns and fears, they lose their power and are easier to release. Once you let go of old habits of thoughts and feelings, you become free to turn your attention away from the past and to focus on creating the future you would like for yourself and for your world.

The veils between heaven and earth are thinner now. This means that the desires of your heart and the focus of your mind can bring about the manifestation of that which is in your highest good. Your thoughts are now creating your present and future reality.

Whatever you focus on increases in energy, so it becomes the dominant force in your world. You can choose to focus on the good, the beautiful and the love inherent in all things. Or you can choose to increase the levels of fear inside you. If you begin to look for good, you will find it. And the more you look for the good in your world, the more it will increase because you are giving it energy by your focus.

You will also begin to notice that you feel more loving, more peaceful and more optimistic. People will seem much nicer to you. Your daily struggle will become less. All this is possible because you begin to look for and focus on the good, and are willing to have more love and harmony in your life. It will seem like a miracle, but miracles are available to all who will receive them.

The Angels are also available to you now in a way that was never possible before. We will assist this entire process of changing the way you perceive your world, if you but ask us. Your thoughts are prayers flowing out into the ethers and bring to you that which you focus on. What do you have to lose by calling on your guardian Angel and asking for more love, peace and harmony in your life? What could it hurt to ask to see that which is good, instead of that which causes pain? There is an incredible simplicity in the truth of universal law. You do not have to be alone in your struggle. Angelic assistance is always available to you, here to bring love and light to the world. Our message is always one of peace and harmony. We seek to bring only good into your life.

Entertain the possibility that what we are saying may actually be true; that what you think about can create your future reality. Notice your thought patterns throughout the day. Is this what you want in your future? Begin to focus your thoughts only on that which you want in your life. When you notice negativity in your mind, say "that is not an acceptable reality, this is what I do want...more love, greater abundance, harmony in my relationships and beauty in my world." Before long you will notice the changes in your life, as that which you ask for manifests. These changes are the new dimensions of love promised to you. You are the one that holds the key to your future by what you are thinking today.

Remember your message from the angels today is:

be willing to face the fears of the past and move into new dimensions of love.

The Gabriel Messages #34

Gratitude opens the door to feeling God's Love.

Dear One,

When you feel God's love, there is a sense of peace and harmony within you. This feeling allows you to step back from the drama in your life, and to let the love of God flow into every situation. When Divine Love is flowing freely through you, miraculous healings occur.

There is one place where you can always go to feel God's love, and that is in your heart. Gratitude is the attitude that will take you into your heart. It does not matter if you see nothing in your life for which to feel grateful, just the act of giving thanks opens a door in your heart to allow God's love in.

When there's nothing else, you can give thanks for just being alive. It is a gift to be in a human body, which is a miraculous instrument. You can give thanks that your heart beats, that your breathing occurs and digestive processes continue without your conscious direction.

If your life feels like a constant struggle, you can give thanks for the lessons you are learning. On the other side of the struggle is freedom. You can give thanks in advance for such freedom.

Prayer shifts our perspective so we can see a larger picture of what is actually going on in our lives. Prayers of gratitude are very powerful, and stimulate an increased flow of God's energy into every situation. This energy can create miraculous change for good. It may take a little effort to find something to be grateful for when you are feeling down, but it will create a beautiful shift in your mind when you do so. This shift is the doorway into a new awareness of the greater truth in your life.

The greater truth is that you are never alone and that you are here on earth to remember your connection to the Divine

Presence in your life. You are meant to live a happy, abundant life with deep fulfillment. In order to do this, it is necessary to step out of the problems life presents and into the flow of God's love, which will bring solutions. It is as if you step through a doorway into right action, trust, and loving awareness. Gratitude is the key that unlocks the door to all you are seeking – a simple thing that brings miracles into your life. Remember:

gratitude opens the door to feeling God's Love.

The Gabriel Messages #35

The release of fear is a small price to pay for the ecstasy of full merging with the Divine.

Dear One,

Having come to a time of decision, you want to make the right one. You know that what you decide will carry on and you are concerned and even fearful of the "what ifs." The only way you can truly make decisions that will best serve you now and in your future is to come to a place of peace and calm within. And this means being in harmony with your Higher Self.

It is from this place that you will make decisions that are for the highest good of all concerned. When you bring fear into your decision-making process it limits you by preventing the full expansiveness of the Divine Mind from working within your conscious mind. It is this merging with God that enables you to feel free, whole and open enough to receive that which is right and true for your life at this time.

No matter how difficult it seems, it is very important that you learn to release the fear that constricts your thinking and actions. Where your attention goes, energy flows. When you focus on the fears, problems and the "what ifs" of your future life, this focused energy magnifies your fearful state. It becomes ever more powerful and can even take over your world – if you allow it to do so. Instead, put your energy into the creation of that wondrous state of being that will best serve you.

The first step in doing this is to breathe deeply and know in your heart that you are being divinely guided at this moment and at every moment in your life. Prayer is also helpful in adjusting your attitude and opening yourself to truth. You can say, "I surrender this fear to God, and I allow the One Mind to work in all my decisions." Even if you still have the feeling of fear in the pit of your stomach, the simple act of praying for release will start you on the path to right decision-making, and will open you to your highest good. Yet often it takes a short while for the physical body to catch up with the mental processes, so it is important to give yourself sufficient time to come to a point of relaxation and expansion before actually making your decisions.

Practice

Take several relaxing, balanced breaths. As you sit in this peaceful moment, allow your exhaled breath to drop heavily like a stone, down below your feet, into the depths of the earth. This will take the frantic energy from your mind and give you greater clarity.

As you inhale see yourself expanding with the pure light of God. See it clearing your mind and calming your heart as you connect with your divine nature. Now replace the fearful thoughts that so pervade your worldly consciousness with images of what you really want in your personal and professional life – images of radiant health, harmony in relationships, abundant cash flow, peace within your own heart. Allow these images of your greater good to permeate your being. Then give thanks for receiving them into your life.

Because you have been trained to be fearful and to worry, even though it is not productive, it takes practice to release the fear and to merge with your true divine nature. The Angels are here to help you do this, enfolding you in wings of pure light and guiding your way to peaceful living.

So ask and you will receive. Allow yourself to be open to the Divine Good, and to be receptive to all the beauty and truth within and around you, so that this good can begin to manifest and work though out your world. If the bounty of the universe is what you want in your life, all you have to do is to let go of the fear that limits you, and allow the grace of God to work for you. After all:

the release of fear is a small price to pay for the ecstasy of full merging with the Divine.

The Gabriel Messages #36

It's safe to let your Light shine!

Dear One,

At the very heart of you is the pure light of God. This light has the ability to change your thinking and change your outer world. It is a light, which like a flame when fanned, can fill every cell, every fiber of your being and transform you. Fanning this flame means giving the light within you a time of focused attention.

Your imagination holds the key to transforming your life. What you believe can be achieved. Even before you believe something is true, you can allow the possibility to be there and imagine it to be true. Wherever you focus your attention, your life-force energy will follow.

Practice

Imagine the light within you shining brightly. Give yourself a moment to inhale deeply and as you exhale, imagine a golden light beam moving from the base of your spine into the earth. As you continue to breathe, feel this deep connection to the earth relax you and provide a strong base within you. Now, bring your attention to your heart center, the energy-field in the middle of your chest. Imagine there is a glowing flame of light burning there. As you breathe in, this flame grows larger and brighter. As you breathe out, the light from this flame begins to fill your body. Continue to breathe and imagine this light expanding behind your shoulders and down your back, feel it filling every organ and every cell. This is the light of pure spirit, the healing love of God. This light fills you with the Divine presence and radiates from you in waves of love.

Now imagine this light shining from you and blessing your house, the area where you live and the planet. Imagine this loving light blessing all the people you meet today. It's a good feeling to send light to others as well as yourself. This light promotes healing energy in the world around you and in your own body. Peace begins within the heart of each person individually. God's light, shining from the heart of each person on Earth, would bring peace to the planet and transform the world.

It's safe to let your light shine. Maybe when you were a child, it did not feel safe to be who you really were inside – innocent, trusting and filled with the light of love. But the consciousness of the people in the world is beginning to change. Now people everywhere are turning to spirituality as the only place where they can find true peace and happiness. They are longing for more sweetness and love in their lives. So the Angels say, "fear not." When you shine your love light on the world, you will be a loving presence. You don't have to say anything. Your energy alone will have a transforming effect.

The visualization of the flame of love in your heart shining out to the people of earth is very potent. No matter what is happening around you, keep this visualization moving through you. It takes a little practice, but will have a healing affect even if you can't see it. Just your willingness to imagine it is enough to create a light shining from within you. This light is that which connects you and everyone around you to the infinite power of Divine Love.

The Master Jesus suggested that your light should not be hidden under a bushel. Let your light shine forth to bless the world and your life for the good.

Remember your message for today,

it's safe to let your Light shine!

The Gabriel Messages #37

Accept that you are a Radiant Spirit of Light who is growing stronger every day in patterns of wholeness and truth.

Dear One,

You are radiant spirit. This is your essence, your connection to the God Source. This is the part of you that never dies, that lives in oneness with all that is, was and ever shall be. When you recognize the truth of your pure essence, and remember this, your daily life can take on a lighter quality. You will be able to look at each situation from a more expanded perspective.

Who you are is a wondrous being growing towards wholeness, peace within and joy-filled awareness. Through this growth, you are finding there is an ultimate truth that runs like a strong current throughout your life. This truth leads you homeward to that place within you where God dwells eternally.

As you hold to this radiant truth, old patterns of thought begin to drop away. You respond more honestly to life in the moment, rather than reacting from old patterns of thought that no longer serve you. As fear and self-doubt cease to run your thinking processes, a radiant presence emerges - your true self, the one who is in harmony with all life.

You are courageously moving toward the light that you know to be ultimate truth. You feel yourself growing stronger in the new patterns of thought you now embrace, thoughts that encourage love and peace within you.

It is a time of profound change on the planet. You are recognizing the need to find the still, peaceful center within you to come back to when the world becomes tumultuous. Every day you receive glimpses of this place, so it becomes easier to access. You know that with practice and a clear intention to find peace within, this will occur.

Courageously you look beyond surface appearances of craziness in your world, and ask for the peace of God to be your only reality. As you do this, a new world opens - a world where miracles become normal and the wings of Angels are ever present to enfold you in love.

Hold to this place of peace within you. Allow yourself to receive guidance and wisdom from the powerful light-filled Presence that is God working in your life, and know the truth of your message from the Angels today:

Accept that you are a Radiant Spirit of Light who is growing stronger every day in patterns of wholeness and truth.

The Gabriel Messages #38

Trust in yourself, and trust in the Angelic Energy working though you.

Dear One,

As the light within you grows stronger and brighter, you will find yourself bringing more wisdom and love to your world. You will begin to trust more deeply in yourself and know you are divinely guided at every moment.

Trust is an energy that grows the more you use it. Like a muscle that strengthens with exercise, so it is with trust. It comes not from the power of your doing, as much as it is an allowing of energy to flow through your being.

Trust comes from a deep level of faith. At the core of your being you know there is a Higher Power at work. You can turn your life over to this Higher Power and things will begin to move in positive directions. Learn to listen more to your intuition than to what society tells you is true. Learn to listen to the voice of your higher self, which is your connecting link to the Divine Source. Remember that you know, deep within, what is best for you. Your higher self knows the answers to all the questions you ask.

Trust the Angels to help you with this process of connecting to God within you. They are an incredible resource awaiting your invitation. Begin to ask your guardian Angel for help in small ways. Follow the guidance you receive and you will find yourself trusting ever more deeply in this wondrous energy working through you. You will notice your life becoming simpler, and everyday activities becoming easier, due to an ever-increasing compassion and clarity within, and due to the grace of the Angels. This grace blesses every step you take and every word you say. This grace also becomes stronger the more you allow it to work in your life. It is a gift for you, but first you must ask, and then you must allow yourself to be open to receiving the good available to you.

These simple acts of trust can transform your world. Remember, your direct link to Divine Grace strengthens when you:

Trust in yourself, and trust in the Angelic Energy working through you.

The Gabriel Messages #39

Give Yourself a Fast from Negative Thoughts about Yourself.

Dear One,

You are being asked to give yourself a fast from negative thoughts about who you think you are. Nothing wears down your sense of self more than this type of negative thinking. It is debilitating in every way. This is a good place to start in order to affect other areas of your life.

A fast is a time period in which you refrain from some activity. Most people are familiar with a food fast, which allows the digestive system a period of recovery. The same is true for a mental fast. It gives your mind time to recover so you can begin to see the truth in your life without judgment.

The judgmental mind is relentless, constantly seeking out inadequacies to bring them to your awareness. Although shining light into the dark corners of your mind is beneficial, bombarding yourself with negative thoughts, even if you believe them to be true, serves no good purpose.

Practice

So what can you do when such incessant thoughts begin in your mind – for example "I should have done better," "I can never do it right," and other negative impressions of your personal character?

Go to God first. Ask to know the truth clearly within yourself. Call on the Angels to illuminate your mind with love and light. Ask for peace in your heart and then offer all your thoughts to the Divine Mind.

During your meditations and prayers, take time to visualize these as limiting thoughts you no longer need. Place them in a box and do something creative with them. Sink them to the bottom of the ocean. Send them to heaven in a colorful balloon. Explode them or put them on a shelf somewhere in your mind's attic. Find an image that works for you and purposefully send the negative thoughts out of your conscious mind.

It is a law of nature that empty spaces become quickly filled, so remember to fill your now empty mind with light. Light is love energy from the Source of all life. Light contains the seeds of truth and will stimulate loving thoughts. You can elaborate on this by imagining that your mind is a golden chalice being filled with God's love.

Repeat this entire process as often as needed until you are no longer willing to tear yourself down and treat yourself unkindly. Instead, see yourself as you truly are – a beloved child of God; a spirit in human form; a clear vessel able to hold the highest possible level of truth; a beautiful, loving being shining love into the world.

You can also turn these statements of truth into affirmations or statements of "I am" and they will become potent reminders, enabling you to strengthen you connection to your divine essence. There is great power in the words "I am". You can substitute these or similar affirmations whenever you notice your mind engaged in negative self-talk. Here are some examples:

I am one with God. I am peaceful and loving. I am inspired with thoughts that serve my highest good. I am relaxed and at peace. I am enjoying an abundant lifestyle using my talents and skills in all I do. I am offering all my work to the Divine Presence and I am fulfilled. All is well.

Have these or other phrases ready to quickly turn to, as soon as you notice negative thoughts creeping in. Don't worry if you don't believe your words at first. This is just the resistance of old habits of thought and these habits can be changed.

Begin now to treat yourself with kindness and compassion. Remember that you are profoundly loved. Know that Angels embrace you in wings of pure light and see you as a beautiful, radiant spirit here to bring love to the world. This is who you really are, so please remember your guidance for today:

give yourself a fast from negative thoughts about yourself.

The Gabriel Messages #40

*Trust in the universal flow of good and know there is a
Perfect Outworking in all situations.*

Dear One,

The Divine Presence is an omnipotent energy, everywhere
present with an infinite capacity for good. This energy flows
through you and surrounds you at all times. There is never a time
when you are not a part of this energy flow of God, which is
Divine Love. In this you can place your trust. You can also be
assured that regardless of where you are or what the situation is,
all energies flow to the highest good for all concerned, at all
times.

Practice

You can set an intention in your mind or on paper for what you
want to see manifest in your life. This gives direction to the
universal flow of energy. It's like holding a vision of your target
in your mind, and then taking aim with a bow and arrow. When
you release the arrow, you trust it will go where you aim it. The
power of God is the energy behind the release of the arrow, but
you are the one who takes aim. When you clearly know what
qualities you want in your life, this Universal energy will flow
where you want it, following the direction of your intention.

The qualities we refer to are qualities of consciousness – like
peace, love, harmony, joy, divine order and abundance. All these
words have been used to describe qualities of the Higher Power
and as they manifest through the universal flow of energy in your
life, they create the perfect outworking of your soul's expression
in every situation.

God wants you to experience happiness, love and all that is
good. You have a divine right to ask for these qualities to

manifest. Regardless of your circumstance, begin now to be very clear about what qualities you want in your life. Write them down. Post them in a place where you will be reminded. You can set the course for your life in this way. Review your intentions often and remain aware of them when circumstances seem upsetting. It is in those moments of upset that you can clearly ask for divine order and harmony to manifest. After that, you need to let go and trust.

The grace of God is available to all who ask and know what qualities they want to manifest in their lives. Remember your guidance for today:

trust in the universal flow of good and know there is a Perfect Outworking in all situations.

The Gabriel Messages #41

A disruption of energy serves to bring clarity – bless it.

Dear One,

Just as a storm can clear the air with its cleansing rain, a disruption of energy also serves to bring clarity.

This disruption is a blessing that may come disguised as that which you do not want in your world. Sometimes knowing what you don't want is the quickest way to knowing what you do want for yourself in all situations. Clarity of mind is necessary in order to bring about that which you would like to see manifested in every area of your life.

Daily life is the cosmic educational system. Every disruption of energy has something to teach. You are here to learn and to grow from your experiences. It's important to remember that it is possible to learn from Joy as well as pain. This is your choice.

A disruption of the status quo creates change. Though change is often uncomfortable, it is intended to bring you continually closer to God. This is your larger life goal, and it's helpful to remember this "bigger picture" when changes occur. It is often the energy from a disruptive circumstance that can propel you to your greater good. Changes are upsetting because you do not know what is coming into your life and this may cause you to feel fearful. But please remember that whatever comes to you can be a significant opportunity for spiritual growth and that you have Angels to walk with you through these changing times.

You can ask for what you want. Claim the greater good that will come from the disruption that has occurred. Ask for the perfect outworking for all concerned in any situation. When you desire that which is for the highest good of all, you set in motion the forces of the universe to support you. Every need is miraculously provided for.

So when upsets happen, bless them. Write them down, place your hand over the writing and imagine brilliant, divine light, which is God's healing energy, working through the situation. Claim Divine Order and know that God and the Angels are available to assist in a perfect outpouring of the highest good of all concerned.

Remember your message from the Angels today:

A disruption of energy serves to bring clarity – bless it.

The Gabriel Messages #42

Pray to remove all obstacles to the Source of all Light.

Dear One,

When you pray to remove all obstacles, you are expressing your desire for full communion with God. You are asking for all that is in the way of your connection with the Divine Presence to be removed, so that you can consciously feel your alignment with love.

God is your partner in life. Prayer is the key to remind you of this partnership. Prayer is a deep and powerful action bringing you into the right frame of mind so your life will work for you in happier ways. Prayer is a tool for opening your heart. It brings love into every situation. Love is the greatest healing energy that exists in the world, so it serves you well to bring love into your life in a conscious way through prayer.

True communion with Spirit is a state of enlightenment. It is fully loving, courageous, free and filled with joy. It is the happy state of knowing that the Divine Presence is always there to turn to so you never feel alone.

When you achieve the conscious awareness of your oneness with God, you will look at life from a state of joy, not fear. You will feel a sense of peace within you. In this state of Divine communion, your true freedom exists.

Pray with your heart, open your mind and be willing for miraculous changes to take place in your life. You were meant to be happy and at peace. You deserve all that is good. Know that you are a beloved child of the Source of all Light.

It is possible to live in love and full communion with God. The Angels are assisting you to make this deep connection at all times. You can call upon their grace to make joy your ever-present reality.

To have more harmony within yourself today, remember this simple suggestion:

pray to remove all obstacles to the Source of all Light.

The Gabriel Messages #43

Accept what is and allow change to occur around you without attachment.

Dear One,

When we suggest for you to accept what is, we mean to be lovingly aware of all situations occurring in and around you – both personally and globally. This means to accept the appearance of what is occurring, without judgment. There is a greater truth underlying all things, no matter how it appears. When you accept a situation as it is, it allows you to release any attachment to having it be different. It is this attachment that can cause you pain.

Just as a child grows and blossoms when in an atmosphere of acceptance and love, so does our world become more expansive and creative when we bring to it this energy of acceptance. When we try to force a child to do what we want, when we have great attachment to his or her behavior conforming to our idea of what is appropriate, the child's energy is restricted. There is no freedom to express the expansiveness of individual creativity.

This also happens to the adult. When there is too much judgment about behaviors and actions in the world, there can be no free-flowing expression of the creativity and love inherent within each person. This does not mean to be tolerant of behavior that is destructive. It means to be aware of the way things appear, to remember the greater truth, to ask for the qualities we would prefer to have manifest, and then to release our attachment. This allows God and the Angels to begin to work in and through all things.

When you release a person or a situation to Spirit, you allow them to be in the Divine Flow taking them to their highest good. Know that even though you have prayed for the greater good, you do not know precisely what this will look like. This is where faith comes in. No matter how something appears, if you have prayed, that prayer is being answered. It does not assist things for you to be attached to the outcome. Know that Infinite Intelligence is working, creating change in the direction of balance and harmony. If there is more that you can do, trust that you will be guided to know this through your intuition.

Acceptance and allowance are two of the greatest powers available to you. These two energies free you to live in the expansiveness that is your divine birthright. When you have an expanded perspective about life, there is greater freedom to express the dynamic, creative qualities inherent within you. There is greater love, for yourself and for all others. You also will feel connected to your Higher Self, which brings about great joy. It is as the Master Jesus said, "know the truth, and the truth will set you free."

Remember your message from the Angels today:

accept what is and allow change to occur around you without attachment.

The Gabriel Messages #44

No one has power over you unless you allow it to happen.

Dear One,

When you are in a situation where you begin to feel powerless and less than another, this can be viewed as a wake up call. We are referring here to any situation in which you feel devalued, not necessarily one of obvious abuse.

If there is another person who wants to have a certain level of power over you, consciously or unconsciously, your physical body is often a good indicator that something is not right. You may notice a feeling of discomfort in your solar plexus area. Perhaps a weight descends on your shoulders and your head hangs down. Paying attention to your bodily discomfort can help you become aware and allow you to disengage yourself from the situation. When you feel strong in yourself, you are less likely to stay in situations that may harm you, or allow others to treat you with disrespect. You do not have to stay in places or around people who do not give you the respect you deserve. However it is also not necessary to react in anger. As much as possible, bless the person or people involved and remove yourself from the situation.

When you feel strong within, good about yourself and generally centered, the area of your solar plexus is filled with energy. When you begin to feel drained, that is literally what is happening to you. When we say no one has power over you unless you allow it to happen, this is the first place where your power is given away. It is now time to take it back.

Sometimes people become so used to being devalued, disempowered and talked down to, they accept this as a natural state. It is not. Every soul on earth deserves to be treated with respect.

In order to stay strong in yourself, steps must be taken so that you feel your inner power, that connection to the light of Pure Spirit that is within you. The solar plexus is the area most affected by the power maneuvers of another person, so the following visualization is helpful in achieving and maintaining your own center of balance.

Practice

Breathe with conscious awareness into the area from your rib cage to below your navel. Imagine this area filled with the glow of a huge sun and allow this bright, golden light to radiate out from this place within you and to fill your entire being. Then see or feel this light moving from the base of your spine into the earth, so you can be connected to that rich, nurturing and grounding presence. Continue visualizing the golden light of the sun filling your solar plexus, centering you with a clear, steadying power that will allow you to take the necessary steps to care for yourself. With practice you can draw on the calming power of this light and the steadying power of the earth whenever needed.

Begin today to respect yourself. Know that you are a radiant child of God and that you have purpose, presence and connection to all the love in the universe. Call on your guardian Angels at all times and know that you are guided and protected by Divine Light. Begin to know your personal connection to a Higher Power, the true power containing all the energy you need to do whatever is required in your life. Fill yourself with the golden light of the sun and feel the nurturing presence of the earth beneath your feet. Reclaim your true power and remember you are never alone.

Your message from the Angels today is:

no one has power over you unless you allow it to happen.

The Gabriel Messages #45

Your job is to have no attachment to the appearance of disharmony but to hold to the love within all things.

Dear One,

Deep within you, and all around you is Divine Love. When you are free from distracting thoughts about the surface appearance of the world, it is easier to remember this truth. Even if you are in a situation that appears to be upsetting, know deeply in your heart that God's Love exists within all things. When you remember this higher wisdom, the outer world of appearances has no choice but to fall in line with your focus of attention.

It has become a scientific truth in the study of quantum physics that the particles of atomic fields arrange themselves into form when the focus of the scientist's attention is there. Before this focus of attention, the particles were waves of energy with unlimited potential. Many books have been written which describe this process in detail. This field of unlimited potential, waiting for your focus of attention, is why your thoughts are so powerful. This is why you can create your new reality by holding a vision of what you want to see happen.

Practice

The Universe will be creating your reality according to your thoughts, whether you are paying attention or not, so having a conscious awareness of the future reality you choose to create is very potent. Imagine a world of love in your thoughts, focus your attention on this as truth, and you shall have it. Know that with God all things are possible. This means it is possible for the world to live in peace and harmony, for all people to have enough food to be healthy, and that all can live in joy-filled abundance. Despite appearances to the contrary, this is Divine will for all human beings.

Your deepest beliefs will affect this process. It is good to be aware of the subconscious thoughts that run contrary to your future visions. Your thoughts are the vehicle to create a world of love and peace for yourself and all others. Know that the greatest truths of the universe are that God exists in all circumstances and Divine Love is within all things. Hold your mind on the power of God's Love, ask for a miracle if you need it, and allow this Universe of Love to show you a reality where harmony and beauty are all that exist.

Remember:

your job is to have no attachment to the appearance of disharmony but to hold to the Love within all things.

The Gabriel Messages #46

Walk in beauty, Live in trust, and know the benevolent love of God guides your way.

Dear One,

These words clarify the way to a carefree, joy-filled and peaceful life.

Walking in beauty means to look at all you see with your heart and mind. This might mean to see beyond the surface appearance of disharmony and know there is perfection and beauty within a situation. There is beauty all around you and sometimes it takes a prayer such as "let me see the beauty here, Angels," to make this apparent.

Walking in beauty also means to allow the awareness that there is beauty in this world to bubble to the surface, so you can be conscious of the great beauty of God's creation. One flower holds as much of the key to universal knowledge as does a whole field of flowers.

Do all you can to be aware of the beauty around you and to bring more beauty into your world. Bringing that one flower into your home can brighten the day, as the spiritual essence in that flower permeates your world. Look for beauty every day and be grateful for all that you find.

Living in trust means that deep within there is an inner knowing that you are never alone, and that the Angels are working for you in your life. As you give your life to God and pray that Divine will be done, you can trust in the appropriate outworking in every situation for the highest good of all concerned. Living in trust means accepting what is apparent in your life, and making a claim for the Divine Order inherent in every situation. Living in trust allows the Angels to comfort and inspire you so you can receive support in every area of your life.

When you know the benevolent love of God guides your way, there is a beacon of light to follow. This love is the most powerful force for good in the universe. This love creates peace and harmony in the heart and soul of each person who remembers. Allow faith in this statement to permeate every cell of your being. You are always guided by God's love and you are never alone. You can call on this love at any time and know truly it is there for you.

So allow this statement to become your way of life. Belief will create more love, joy and peace for you in every way.

Again dear one we say to you:

walk in beauty, live in trust and know the benevolent love of God guides your way.

The Gabriel Messages #47

All situations are opportunities for the Divine Light to shine through you as times of celebration, not fear.

Dear One,

Your life is divinely guided and directed at every moment. Calling on the Angels for assistance gives you a direct link to your greater good and aids the wisdom of the universe to flow through you. When you dwell in fear or doubt, this constricts your perception and does not allow the natural out-flowing of good to come through you into your world. Whatever situation is occurring in your life, allow the Divine Light to show you the possibility for good. Ask for a perfect outworking of the highest good for all concerned. This will open the door for the Angelic forces to begin their work. Receiving the assistance of the Angels is truly a cause for celebration. Celebrate the fact that you are not alone. Celebrate the fact that all you do is now divinely guided, because you asked.

You can believe you have to do it all by yourself if you choose. However, with even the smallest intention to receive help, with the slightest hope that good can come of the situations in your life, with the willingness to release the fear that entraps you, light will flow to you in abundance. This will bring inspiration and guidance for your next steps, and will allow you to actually do that which will be in your highest good. You are the one who takes the steps, no one can do this for you. But when you walk, you will be held in the arms of the Angels of Light. We are asking you to walk in trust and faith.

We are also asking you to be clear about your intentions for your life. These intentions have the power to create your world. When you know which qualities you want to have, you should ask for them directly. Do you want more love in your life? Or peace in your heart? Or financial abundance so you can live with more freedom? Ask for these qualities and give yourself the time to breathe them into your being. Breathe them in and then walk in the trust that you will be supported for your highest good. Then take the steps you are inspired to take, knowing you are being guided every step of the way. Have faith in the Divine Light that will never leave you. It can only grow stronger every time you imagine that you are surrounded by it.

Your imagination carries the key to your future. Imagine only that which you want to fulfill your life. Give no energy to fearful thoughts. Love is the only truth. You are being blessed now with the light of the Angels, the holy messengers of God's love.

Call on your guardian Angel often and never doubt this presence in your life. Know that whatever situation you are experiencing can be transformed by the power of Divine Light. Receive this light and celebrate.

Remember your message from the Angels today:

all situations are opportunities for the Divine Light to shine through you as times of celebration not fear.

The Gabriel Messages #48

Allow the grace of the Angels to work in everyday functions.

Dear One,

The Angels are always available. Their presence is blessing all that you do and say. Their intention is toward Peace, Harmony and Divine Order. When you call upon the grace of the Angels, all situations are blessed with their intentional energy. This is a very powerful tool to use in daily life.

Do you want order in your work place so that all your work is done quickly and easily, so that all you need is available, and all your words and actions are guided? If so, call the Angels into your work place. Ask for their blessings and know divine order will be the result. Allow the Angels to intervene on your behalf even with the smallest details that you feel you should take care of by yourself. You will find your work flowing more easily and smoothly. Even more, Creative Solutions will abound.

Do you want peace and harmony in your relationships? Ask the Angels to assist in your family and in all interactions with others. More harmony and a new level of grace will be the result.

The Angels are here to bring more love, harmony and order into daily life. They are here to demonstrate how much easier life can be when you allow a greater level of energy to work through you. But they will not intervene unless they are asked, so there must be a willingness on your part to bring peace-filled energy into your life.

The Angels are messengers of God. They are not here to be worshipped or to gain power over you. They are here to assist you. They are a part of the Divine Spirit just as humans are, so there is no need to fear when your intention is to have more miracles in your life. Your willingness to have more love, joy and harmony will bring to you those very qualities you seek. You can bring the Angels into your life to assist you in enhancing the energy you work with every day.

It is a great gift to have the Angels offering their energy for planetary good, as well as for the good of your personal life. Allow yourself to receive this blessing. Ask for assistance in all the mundane things that bring you stress. Ask for angelic intervention in all overwhelming situations. Allow yourself to feel this incredible level of support. Be willing to have yourself surrounded in wings of pure love and see how much easier your life will feel to you. Receive the love, light and wisdom of the Angels now. And remember your message today:

allow the grace of the Angels to work in every day functions.

The Gabriel Messages#49

The teachers you seek are love and wisdom. They are within you.

Dear One,

You have within you all the love and wisdom you need to be whole and live in a holy way in the world. Each time you seek outside yourself for these qualities you find a little more of your confidence and self-esteem slipping away.

This is not to say that you should not seek advice from others. But when this advice is received, there must be a time of reflection before you act on it. When advice is appropriate for you to act on, there will be a sense of resonance within you, a little feeling of rightness, if not a whole hearted "Yes!"

Sensitivity to this resonance can be developed. Pray to know what is in your highest good beyond a shadow of a doubt, and be willing to act when this knowing is clear. This is taking responsibility for your life, and will pay off in large future dividends as you begin to know the truth within yourself, and act accordingly.

Looking to others for your truth throws your whole body out of balance. Energy moves into the head as you strain to listen only with the mind and not the heart or your gut. The old wives' tale about "gut-level knowing" is extremely valuable. This way of knowing goes beyond common sense, to an uncommon sense of what is right for you. No one else can tell you what is right for you. Pray to know your own Truth.

This is a time of change on the planet. Many are finding that the old ways no longer work. Businesses are struggling, so are families, relationships, and governments. It seems the challenges are so large that the answers are unclear. We can know that if we were enlightened enough in any situation, we would see that there is always an inspired and creative solution. We can affirm and pray for this in the world, as well as within our own lives.

All that goes on in our outer world is only a reflection of our inner world. So when we begin trusting our own answers within, these small steps will lead to leaping bounds in our lives. We have spoken of the resonance available within when others speak to you of what they believe is correct action for you to take. This same inner knowing is the mechanism to be used when you look to your own inner guidance.

Take the time to stop and breathe, before acting. The breath holds the connection to Divine Guidance. Experience this feeling now, as your energy field expands along with your body when you breathe deeply. Feel your feet on the earth and the connecting link from your head to your feet. As you do this, you become a bridge from Heaven to Earth.

Now you are ready to listen to the truth and wisdom within you, and remember your message from the Angels today:

the teachers you seek are love and wisdom. They are within you.

The Gabriel Messages #50

Praise God and praise yourself for the path you have chosen.

Dear One,

Your path in life is decided upon before you take birth in human form. Your soul reviews the lessons necessary for highest growth, and then chooses those life experiences that will provide them. From a human perspective, this choice is often difficult to comprehend. Many outwardly horrendous lifetimes have powerful lessons though they may be beyond human understanding.

To truly understand the soul's growth, it is necessary to have an expanded perspective that sees an overall picture. When situations occur in life that seem very difficult to handle, a certain balance is provided in knowing that, on a soul level, a great learning experience is occurring and that you are given all you need to handle the situation, for the highest good of all concerned.

This does not mean that your emotions do not exist, or that somehow you should not feel upset, because in human terms your experience is very real and your feelings valid. Within the power of your soul, however, there is a great gift in your situation. No matter how senseless a condition may appear to your human eyes, a greater truth is available. It can assist you to remember this and to pray to see it. It can also help to remember that you live in a benevolent universe where the grace of God is available at all times.

From a human perspective, it is also often difficult to experience incredible joy and happiness. There are many people in your world who say: "it's too good to be true, watch out when things get too good," etc. The Angels say to you that you are a beloved child of God who deserves to be happy and to have incredible blessings in your life. If this is what you are experiencing right now, enjoy it. Live this blessed moment to the fullest. Never doubt that good things happen, and that joy and miracles are the natural state of being.

Do not doubt the path you have chosen. If there is something in your world that you want to change, pray that it be transformed for the highest good of all concerned. Trust in your Angelic teachers and in God's presence, which is eternally within you. Be grateful for your life and most of all:

praise God and praise yourself for the path you have chosen.

The Gabriel Messages #51

*Acknowledge yourself for how far you have come
instead of how far you think you have to go.*

Dear One,

You have grown and changed so much. You are so busy being in the moment, applying all you have learned, and giving of your talents, that it's necessary to take time to really notice how far you have come.

See all that you have given to others and your world. Notice how much you have changed and how hard you have worked on yourself. See how your intention for a better life is leading you forward. You have come a long way and truly have so much to offer. For all that you are, acknowledge yourself.

Acknowledge your commitment to a higher purpose in life. Acknowledge your willingness to give. Acknowledge yourself for the loving heart you share so freely, asking little in return.

It is easy to be caught up in the world's view of goals and achievements. This spurs you to look forward to the future and to hurry through the present. In order to be more integrated and whole as a person, it is also necessary to look honestly at the past. This means being compassionate with yourself, seeing the lessons that you have learned, the things you would do differently, and knowing you have done the best you could. Then come into the present moment and acknowledge yourself for how far you have come.

Acknowledge yourself for who you are right now. Know that you are still learning many lessons in life but that you are willing to use all you have learned to live a fulfilling life. Honor the Spirit within you, honor the Love in your heart, respect the person you are right now and know the Angels of God are guiding you in every moment.

When you treat yourself with honor and respect, the doors of Heaven open for you to fulfill your highest destiny on earth and to live in peace.

Remember to:

acknowledge yourself for how far you have come instead of how far you have to go.

The Gabriel Messages #52

You would not have the desire without the means of fulfilling it.

Dear One,

All things in life are a part of the Higher Power. This includes the desires of your heart. You have within you all that it takes to fulfill these desires and create the life you want to have. Know that each time you feel a deep longing, the seed of fulfillment is inherent within it.

There is a deep re-awakening within you, showing you a potential for all that you desire. This re-awakening results from your connection to God and the remembrance of the Angels who are guiding you always. As you commune more and more with this energy, your life will begin to take on the magical qualities you desire.

It begins with letting go. When you know in your heart that all your needs will be abundantly met, you can release the part of you that wants acquisition. You will now be free to discover the true desires in your heart. True desires have qualities that are fulfilled when the desires have been manifested. If the desire is for money, there is a quality your heart seeks to have fulfilled – a sense of safety, an abundant lifestyle, or perhaps, simply freedom from worry.

Becoming aware of these qualities allows you to take action to gain these first, which will then allow the material form to manifest in a form which is in your highest good. The first step after discovering the qualities you seek, is always to ask for what you want, making sure you clearly state the qualities you are seeking to have. The Angelic Dimensions stand ready to assist you in the process of gaining all you desire in your life. Clarity is key.

Practice

It is truly God's Plan to have all beings live in a state of abundant joy and freedom from fears, with peace, harmony and love in the world as well as within families. These qualities are not too much to ask for in your prayers because they are the natural state of balance in God's world. Your prayers you offer in order to attain them opens your mind and heart to fulfillment in your personal life.

It is also vital to be in the company of like-minded souls who believe that miracles are not only possible, they are also willing to have them manifest in their own lives. It is clear that in some situations in the world, only a miracle of divine proportions can create a solution. With enough people believing miracles are possible, there is no doubt that creative solutions, which are beyond the mind's ability to understand at this time, will occur.

Begin now to allow miracles to manifest in your world. Be the first one to ask for divine intervention, and to share your belief with others, so that all may live in a new level of conscious awareness and abundant joy.

Those desires in your heart are there to remind you that miracles happen, and God provides you the ways to have all the good you desire in your life. Know that you are blessed and profoundly loved. Call on the Divine Spirit and the Angels then allow the desires of your heart to be fulfilled. Remember:

you would not have the desire without the means of fulfilling it.

The Gabriel Messages #53

One way to balance within is to allow yourself to love and be loved.

Dear One,

When you allow yourself to love another person it opens channels within your being to receive divine love from God, the Infinite Source. There is an inexhaustible supply of this love. When you begin to freely give this love you are blessed with more, so you can continue to give. In this way you will never be starving for love because you feel you have given too much. You cannot give too much love, because the inexhaustible resource of God's love is equal to every demand.

There are many ways to give love. At times the most loving thing you can do is to leave people alone to follow their own path in life. Even then, you are not shutting them out of your heart, although you may never see them again. Giving love freely means loving yourself enough to only be in those situations which serve your highest good at all times, and which allow you to be treated in a respectful manner.

Receiving love is sometimes more difficult than giving it, but your willingness to receive is also necessary for perfect balance to exist in your life. When you receive love from others, you are allowing them to give. This completes the circuit of Divine Love. Allowing yourself to be loved opens the door to receiving infinite abundance from the universe, and creates channels for you to receive in wondrous ways from other people. This means receiving support for your life, which is important because you were never meant to struggle alone. You are a child of God, and so are given infinite ways to receive love. Allow yourself to receive and be grateful for all the demonstrations of love, large and small, which are given to you every day.

When you open your heart to another person it creates an energy of love within you which in turn brings balance to all the systems of the physical body. When your body is in balance, it creates healing currents within itself. This is one reason that love is such a powerful healing force. To have health in your body, you cannot allow yourself to shut down your heart to another.

When the quality of balance is active in your life, all things will seem to fall into perfect order. There will be balance in your finances, in your health, in your household, and in your spiritual life. When you give and receive in a balanced way you are open to the flow of Divine energy that gives depth, beauty and meaning to your life. You will feel abundantly blessed in every way.

Practice

It is important to have the "energy of allowing" actively influencing your life. When you allow things to happen for you, there is no feeling of pushing "the river of life." You take one step and the way is open for the next, and so it goes without effort. When you push to make things happen, stress is created in your body and mind. This leads to an imbalance that could cause disease. So practice acting in balance and harmony with all life. Allow others to love and support you. It will then become easier to have a more joy-filled, meaningful existence as this sense of allowing will help create the openness necessary for miracles to occur.

Step into the flow of a miraculous lifestyle. Give yourself the opportunity to be loved and supported by God and by those who love you. Let yourself give love freely, and know that it will be returned in miraculous ways. Allow yourself to give love so you will create balance in body, mind and emotions. Know that circumstances work for your highest good when you are in balance with all of life. Remember your message from the angels today:

one way to balance within is to allow yourself to love and be loved.

The Gabriel Messages #54

Make choices for greater Life, Peace and Joy, and all the forces of the Universe align themselves behind you.

Dear Ones,

This is a universe of free will. The Angels will not step in to assist without being asked. "Ask and you shall receive" was the statement of Master Jesus. So it is important to ask for this support in all the choices you make in your life, from moment to moment.

When you make a choice to think in a positive, instead of negative way; when you make a choice to accept, rather than judge, the decisions made by another; when you agree to give instead of waiting to receive; all these choices are examples of opening your heart and mind to receiving your highest good. When you choose the highest good for all, you signal the available energy in the universe to come to your aid. Miracles will occur naturally all around you, by your willingness to receive them. People will suddenly begin to give to you in a different way. Synchronous events will transpire in ways you never thought possible. This is the natural flow of God's grace available to all who are willing to work in harmony with Divine Energy and have the forces of the universe align behind them.

These results also come from a willingness on your part to have your life be good, and to allow others to love and support you. It has to do with knowing what you want and asking for it directly, as well as having faith to know that there is a greater order and good available to all who believe.

So accept that what is occurring around you in your life is a reflection of what is occurring within you. Begin to make small choices to love instead of hate, to forgive the person who has wronged you, even when the action seems unforgivable, to give thanks for what you have instead of complaining about what you don't have, and to believe that miracles can occur in your life, when you are willing to receive them.

These shifts in attitude bring a return of greater love, joy and fulfillment in your life. It all begins with you and with your sincere willingness to allow the Angels and the Divine Spirit to come to your assistance.

So remember your message from the Angels today:

make choices for greater Life, Peace and Joy and all the forces of the Universe align themselves behind you.

The Gabriel Messages #55

Take time to bless that which you have and ask for what you want.

Dear One,

You may be finding yourself in a time of questioning and dissatisfaction with your life. However, this is also a time of great opportunity. Every moment of your conscious awareness creates the qualities of your future moments. You can ask for those qualities you feel are missing from your life now, and they will come to you from your sincere prayer.

It is not about asking for material things. Instead, ask for those qualities of consciousness you believe you would have if you had the things you want. For example, if you want a new job, what qualities would this job give you? Abundant income? Harmonious atmosphere with co-workers? Fulfillment and joy doing that which you love? Perhaps ease in transportation?

When you know the qualities you want, this allows the universe to provide these qualities in a work situation that may be even better than the type of work you were looking for. When you ask for a narrowly defined work environment, you may get exactly what you ask for but the qualities that would make you happy may not be present.

Practice

It's important not to limit the response of the universe to the confines of your present awareness. But if you do choose to be precise, also say, "this or something better, God" and then let go. You can also give thanks in advance for answered prayers by saying, "thank you Spirit for meeting my needs in ways better than I can imagine. Thank you for the Divine Order in this situation."

Blessing situations also brings more good to you. Even if your world appears to be falling apart around you, you can bless the changes occurring and know there is Divine Order beneath the illusion of disharmony.

Though it may not appear that you have much you can bless, you can bless the gift of another day of life. You can bless the learning experiences you are now receiving knowing they are bringing you to a greater good. You can bless the people in your life, knowing they are your perfect teachers for what you need to learn at this time.

Remember to give more attention to what you want than on what you don't have. It seems a small distinction but power is given to whatever you focus your energy upon. If what you are experiencing is not what you want, bless it anyway. But do not dwell there. Shift your focus to ask for whatever good you want – greater happiness, joy-filled relationships, abundant income, satisfying work. Then say, "thank you God" and release your prayers to the universe to be fulfilled. Whenever you think of it, bless your life, say thank you for what you have and want, then let Divine Will take over.

You deserve to be happy and have miracles in your life. A prayerful attitude of blessing and gratitude can bring to you all the good life has to offer. You are worthy to receive the grace of God. All who ask sincerely are answered in kind. Remember your message from the Angels today is:

take time to bless that which you have and ask for what you want.

The Gabriel Messages #56

All that you have learned and all that has happened to you brought you to where you are now. Be grateful.

Dear One,

You have come to a time when acknowledgment of yourself is necessary. There needs to be a truce between the warring factions of your mind. One part of you is diligently watching to make sure that you never make a mistake. When you inevitably do, it leaps to chastise and remind you about all the ways you are wrong. This judgmental mind is never happy with your progress. Nothing you do could ever be good enough. It is relentless in its pursuit of your wrongness. It is time to tell this part of your mind to take a vacation. It needs to lose itself in the beauty of nature, and leave the rest of you alone.

You are on this earth plane to learn. It is by making mistakes that people learn lessons. It is impossible to do things right and perfectly every time. The Divine Presence does not expect this of you. What is necessary is that you follow your heart and your inner guidance. There is much wisdom within you. But it is often like a small voice calling in the wilderness, drowned out by critical and judgmental thoughts. Yet it is listening to this quieter voice that would most serve you in your life. This voice is telling you that you are a child of a loving God, and that there is nothing you can do which could stop the flow of Infinite Love.

There is also society's voice which demands you live up to certain expectations. When you are in alignment with your Higher Self, there is a flow of love-filled energy that allows you to step into a way of being which is totally connected to the Divine Power within and around you. This energy is inviting you to be rather than do. You are being asked to let go of the confining armor of society's expectations and of your judgmental mind that has been conditioned by it. You are being asked to look with compassion upon yourself, and to notice the many things you are learning at this time. It is a powerful time on Earth when, although there is great suffering and fear, there are also incredible opportunities to break through into great love and peace.

Practice

What you see in the world is colored by how you see yourself. Can you see that, in the past, you took the steps that seemed appropriate for you at the time? Do you notice that there were times when your heart told you to make a certain choice, but for various reasons, you did not follow your intuition? All these experiences have assisted you in learning lessons necessary for your growth. It is time to totally forgive yourself for behaving in ways you judge as wrong or bad. You would have made different choices had you known better, but you acted from your awareness at that time. Forgive yourself and get on with your life. Do not waste any more precious time in self-criticism. You are making choices in this moment to create your future. All that you have is this moment. Let the past go, and do not fear the future. Know that you are exactly where you need to be for your perfect lessons in life. It is up to you to lift the mantle of judgment and allow yourself to grow into who you would most like to be.

Imagine acting in ways that bring you joy. Imagine your world surrounded in love. Know that you are a good, honest and caring person and give yourself the loving respect you deserve. Your imagination can set a powerful intention for your life when you use it to visualize a new and more harmonious way to be. When you set an intention, all the forces of the universe align themselves to manifest that which you visualize. It is wise to be careful how you use this powerful tool. You do receive whatever you focus on, if your focus and desire are strong enough. It is a Universal Law.

Remember to be grateful for your life. It is an incredible gift to be in a physical body. With this body you can do so many things to enjoy this world of beauty. Be grateful for all that you are learning now, even if, at times, it feels uncomfortable. Be grateful for all that you have, even if it does not seem to be enough. Gratitude awakens your mind to the greater truth within all things, and lifts your spirit into appreciation and joy.

So remember your message from the Angels today:

all that you have learned and all that has happened to you brought you to where you are now. Be grateful.

BIOGRAPHY

Shanta Gabriel is a gifted author, teacher and healer. Inspired by her many years study of ancient forms of healing, as well as energy transference received from her master teachers, Shanta's gift is the transmission of divine inspiration into everyday life.

Shanta's alignment with the Angelic Dimensions was both unexpected and spontaneous, beginning with visitations from Archangel Michael in 1988, when he filled her healing room with golden light and inspired her powerful form of bodywork, Light Activation Therapy.

In 1990, Archangel Gabriel initiated a transmission of divine, timeless wisdom that resulted in *Angel Messages Book and Card Set*, as well as a wealth of material yet to be published. The new release of *The Gabriel Messages* has been greatly anticipated and is a response to many continuing requests from those whose lives have been enriched and transformed through their own unique connection to this comforting and inspiring work.

On January 1, 2007, Shanta moved to the San Francisco Bay area from Hawaii. A California native, she lived in Hawaii for over 20 years, and credits the islands' warmth and beauty as inspiration for her work. Her dedication to bringing the enlightened perspective of the Angelic Dimensions to earth has strengthened as our world becomes more complex. She continues her work through a seven-month Archangel Study Program, as well as private sessions that include Angel readings as well as hands-on massage combining Hawaiian Lomi Lomi with her Light Activation work. She is available for private readings, workshops and retreats that bridge Heaven and Earth. For more information, see Seminars at www.shantagabriel.com.

BOOKS

O books
O is a symbol of the world, of oneness and unity. In
different cultures it also means the "eye", symbolizing
knowledge and insight, and in Old English it means "place
of love or home". O books explores the many paths of
understanding which different traditions have developed
down the ages, particularly those today that express
respect for the planet and all of life.

For more information on the full list of over 300 titles
please visit our website
www.O-books.net